Social-Emotional Learning in English Language Teaching

BIGs (Brief Instructional Guides)

Social-Emotional Learning in English Language Teaching
Luis Javier Pentón Herrera & Janine J. Darragh

Theory and Practice: Bite-Sized Activities for Teaching Reading Skills
Aviva Katzenell

Refugee Students: What Every ESL Teacher Needs to Know
Jeffra Flaitz

Genre-Based Writing: What Every ESL Teacher Needs to Know
Christine Tardy

Drama in the Language Classroom: What Every ESL Teacher Needs to Know
Carmela Romano Gillette & Deric McNish

Conflict Resolution Training for the Classroom: What Every ESL Teacher Needs to Know
Barrie J. Roberts

Teaching Vocabulary Is the Writing Teacher's Job: Why and How
Keith S. Folse

Academic Word Lists: What Every Teacher Needs to Know
Keith S. Folse

Service-Learning: What Every ESL Teacher Needs to Know
Trisha Dowling & James Perren

SLIFE: What Every Teacher Needs to Know
Andrea DeCapua

Task-Based Listening: What Every ESL Teacher Needs to Know
Steven Brown

The Three Minute Thesis in the Classroom: What Every ESL Teacher Needs to Know
Heather Boldt

Teaching Speaking Online: What Every ESL Teacher Needs to Know
Pamela Bogart

Content-Based Instruction: What Every ESL Teacher Needs to Know
Marguerite Ann Snow & Donna M. Brinton

Flipping the Classroom: What Every ESL Teacher Should Know
Robyn Brinks Lockwood

MOOCs: What Every ESL Teacher Needs to Know
Pamela Bogart

Academic Speaking and the Boundaries of Routinized Lexical Phrases
Susan M. Barone & Summer Dickinson

What Error Correction Can(not) Accomplish for Second Language Writers: Dispelling Myths, Discussing Options
Dana R. Ferris

Social-Emotional Learning in English Language Teaching

By

Luis Javier Pentón Herrera and Janine J. Darragh

University of Michigan Press
Ann Arbor

All rights reserved
Published in the United States of America by the
University of Michigan Press
Manufactured in the United States of America
Printed on acid-free paper

ISBN 978-0-472-03985-2 (print)
ISBN 978-0-472-22212-4 (e-book)

First published December 2024

DEDICATION

We dedicate this book to all the educators who are doing the courageous and necessary work of supporting learners around the world. May your journey into social-emotional learning give you and your students the skills, motivation, and hope needed to build a better world for all.

CONTENTS

LIST OF FIGURES AND TABLES

FIGURES

TABLES

PREFACE

The seed for this book was planted in 2023 in an inspiring collaboration with the U.S. Department of State's English Language Program, where we embarked on creating the 2023 Specialist Master Class (https://www.youtube.com/watch?v=tg5HFugz67w). This endeavor led us to co-write and record a series of six videos focused on social-emotional learning and trauma-sensitive practices (Darragh & Pentón Herrera, 2023). The overwhelming feedback from educators worldwide, gathered through webinars and discussions, highlighted a profound need and appreciation for these topics in our field. However, despite the clear demand, we noticed a significant gap in published materials and resources about these critical topics, especially as they specifically relate to English language teachers. This gap fueled our motivation, becoming the source of energy and inspiration behind the writing of this book.

The book you are now reading was written by, with, and for educators; it is intended for practitioners, curriculum designers, researchers, and stakeholders at large in ELT. We have divided this manuscript into five chapters.

In **Chapter 1: What Is Social-Emotional Learning?**, we introduce the foundational concepts of SEL and its critical importance in the realm of language education. This chapter sets the stage for understanding SEL's role in fostering not only linguistic competence but also emotional intelligence and intercultural understanding among learners.

In **Chapter 2: Why Social-Emotional Learning in Language Teaching?**, we conceptualize SEL, exploring its theoretical underpinnings and the empirical research supporting its integration into language education. This chapter provides readers with a comprehensive understanding of SEL's components and its impact on both teachers and learners.

To bridge theory with practice, we offer in **Chapter 3: How to Include Social-Emotional Learning in Language Teaching**, practical strategies for implementing SEL in language classrooms. Here, educators will find a wealth of activities, teaching approaches, and reflective practices designed to integrate SEL into everyday teaching and learning processes effectively.

In **Chapter 4: Social-Emotional Learning and Responsible Well-Being**, we explore the connection between SEL and collective well-being, highlighting the significance of a supportive educational environment for the holistic development of the educational community.

We end the book with **Chapter 5: Future Directions for Social-Emotional Learning in Language Teaching**, which addresses the potential challenges and opportunities in SEL within ELT and calls for collaborative efforts to innovate and expand SEL practices in language education.

Through this structured approach, the book aims to equip educators, curriculum designers, researchers, and stakeholders in ELT with the knowledge and tools necessary to transform language teaching into a conduit for nurturing compassionate, empathetic, and globally minded individuals.

Thank you for joining us on this journey!

Chapter 1
What Is Social-Emotional Learning?

Brief Overview of Social-Emotional Learning

The origins of the term *social-emotional learning* (SEL) can be traced back to the 1960s, and it is attributed to the efforts of James Comer, a Yale alumnus. Comer was dedicated to exploring strategies to enhance the academic performance of underprivileged children in New Haven, Connecticut (Comer, 1980). He advocated a holistic approach to education, emphasizing the importance of nurturing and engaging learning environments. In such settings, both educators and students could foster significant relationships, contributing to enhanced learning outcomes and school advancement (Comer & Emmons, 2006). Concurrently, there was a growing consensus among scholars about the essentiality of establishing structures that catered to the social and emotional development of students within educational settings. In 1994, a diverse group consisting of researchers, educators, professionals, and child welfare proponents established the Collaborative for Academic, Social, and Emotional Learning (CASEL) and coined the term *social and emotional learning* (CASEL, n.d.). Three years later, the concept of SEL was elaborated in the publication *Promoting Social and Emotional Learning: Guidelines for Educators* (Elias et al., 1997). Since this seminal work, both CASEL's contributions and the implementation of SEL principles have continuously expanded within the educational sphere.

Although CASEL's framework might be one of the most well-known around the world, it is certainly not the only framework or practice for SEL. In the present day, SEL is commonly described as the process by which "children and adults acquire and apply competencies to recognize and manage emotions, set and achieve positive goals, appreciate the perspectives of others, establish and maintain supportive relationships, make responsible decisions, and handle personal and interpersonal situations constructively" (Osher et al., 2016, p. 645). In this definition, the word *process* is of particular importance because it denotes that SEL is not tied down to specific frameworks or practices. Instead, SEL is meant to be a pedagogical approach in which educators look at their students and their environments and implement practices that support their students' social-emotional competencies and intelligence. Quoting Pentón Herrera and Martínez-Alba, "SEL has no limitations; practitioners can modify SEL practices to fit their learning realities, students' necessities, and subjects taught" (2021, p. vii).

The diverse nature of SEL is evidenced by a plethora of practices globally, which, despite embodying the principles of SEL, might not be explicitly labeled as such. For instance, in some educational contexts, practices such as mindfulness meditation, service learning, or restorative justice might not be designated as SEL but inherently promote social and emotional competencies (Durlak et al., 2011). Similarly, in countries like Japan, Lesson Study—a collaborative approach to professional development and improving student learning—aligns with SEL principles without being directly identified as such (Lewis et al., 2006). Furthermore, in Indigenous communities, traditional practices that foster community well-being and individual emotional intelligence mirror SEL objectives, even though they may not employ the contemporary terminology of SEL (Kovats Sánchez et al., 2022). Such practices are illustrative of the intrinsic and universal value of nurturing social and emotional capabilities. These capabilities are foundational for developing holistic individuals who are equipped not just academically, but also socially and emotionally, to navigate the complexities of the contemporary world. The embrace of culturally nuanced SEL expressions enriches educational dialogues, fostering a more diversified, equitable, and comprehensive learning experience for all students (Elias et al., 1997).

Social-Emotional Learning in English Language Teaching

In the English language teaching (ELT) field, SEL, though a burgeoning focus, is not entirely new; its roots are embedded in foundational theories and practices. Concepts like Maslow's hierarchy of needs (1943) and Krashen's affective filter hypothesis (1982) have subtly underscored the essence of social and emotional elements in facilitating effective language learning. In addition, the evolving landscape of our field, which has reflected a gradual shift toward more interactive, learner-centered approaches, has also set a precedent for SEL approaches.

For example, the grammar-translation method, which originated in the early sixteenth century and has long been used to teach language, focuses on written language, meticulous grammar, and translation exercises. This method offers limited scope for the integration of SEL, given its lack of emphasis on social interaction and emotional engagement (Larsen-Freeman & Anderson, 2011). The acknowledgment of the need for language *use*, not just language *practice*, paved the way for the communicative approach, which emerged in the 1970s. The communicative approach emphasized the use of language as a medium for communication, focusing on the functional aspect of language and the ability to express personal meaning (Richards & Rodgers, 2001). Unlike previous traditional methods that prioritized grammatical competence, this approach values interactive and meaningful communication, setting a foundation that naturally aligns with SEL's emphasis on understanding and managing emotions, fostering empathy, and building relationships.

More contemporary approaches and conversations in the field, such as the post-method pedagogies, also challenge the one-size-fits-all approach of traditional methodologies by advocating for context-sensitive, adaptable teaching practices that respond to the unique needs of learners and educational settings (Kumaravadivelu, 2006). This pedagogical stance resonates with SEL's emphasis on tailoring educational experiences to foster personal and social development alongside academic achievement. Integrating SEL principles within post-method pedagogies can further empower educators to design learning environments that support holistic development, encompassing cognitive, emotional, and social growth. While holistic and interactive teaching methods share commonalities with SEL, particularly in their focus on engaging and learner-centered practices, SEL distinguishes itself by explicitly aiming to develop social and emotional competencies. Therefore, not all holistic and interactive teaching can be categorized as SEL, but SEL can enhance these teaching approaches by systematically incorporating strategies that support the development of emotional and social intelligence.

These aforementioned concepts and practices, though not labeled as SEL, resonate with the core principles of social-emotional learning and have the capacity to grow and expand by learning from SEL itself. This intertwining is not a modern integration but has been inherently present, suggesting that the effectiveness of ELT is intrinsically linked to the acknowledgment and incorporation of SEL principles. In this light, the emergence of SEL in ELT signifies a reawakening and formal recognition of what has always been an undercurrent—the indelible imprint of social and emotional factors in shaping and enhancing the language learning journey.

The burgeoning interest in the intersectionality between SEL and ELT is further evidenced by recent studies and dialogues highlighting the multifaceted benefits of SEL. Preliminary inquiries into the integration of SEL in ELT environments have underscored its pivotal role in augmenting both the learners' social-emotional competencies and their academic outcomes (Bai et al., 2021; Soodmand Afshar et al., 2016; Suganda et al., 2018). In tandem, practitioner-oriented discourses (e.g., Martínez-Alba & Pentón Herrera, 2023; McNair & Pentón Herrera, 2022; Pentón Herrera & McNair, 2021; Muller & Pentón Herrera, 2023) reveal an affirming consensus on the positive echoes of SEL integration in ELT, enriching both the learning experience and the teaching dynamics (Pentón Herrera, 2020; Pentón Herrera & Martínez-Alba, 2021). The amplification of SEL's resonance in ELT is not a serendipitous evolution; rather, it is deeply rooted in the enriched learning contexts where social and emotional aspects are valued as driving forces for heightened cognitive engagement and results. In this evolving landscape, SEL is not an extension but is weaving itself as a central thread in the tapestry of ELT, heralding an era in which learning transcends linguistic competence to embrace holistic human development—and this is the purpose and vision of our book.

Building upon this vision, it is imperative to recognize that although SEL is increasingly acknowledged in ELT, a breadth of research and practices already aligns with SEL principles, yet is not explicitly identified as such. Topics spanning the teaching of moral values (Pentón Herrera, 2019), virtues education (Karam, 2021), identity (Yazan, 2019), positive psychology (MacIntyre et al., 2019), emotions (Richards, 2022), drama (McGovern & Yeganeh, 2023), agency (Tao & Gao, 2021), peace education (Birch, 2009, 2022), and well-being (Mercer & Gregersen, 2020; Pentón Herrera et al., 2023a) implicitly resonate with the social and emotional aspects of learning. We propose an integration of these diverse yet interconnected domains under the comprehensive banner of SEL, promoting an inclusive, holistic approach to curriculum development, instructional strategies, and research in ELT. This amalgamation promises a shared lexicon and conceptual framework, fostering a climate of interdisciplinary collaboration and optimized interventions (Pentón Herrera & Martínez-Alba, 2022). The adoption of this comprehensive SEL framework promises not just to bridge conceptual and practical divides but also to elevate the overall educational quality and impact in the realm of ELT.

Furthermore, unifying these diverse educational concepts under the SEL umbrella is poised to enhance systematic curriculum integration, professional development, and policy formulation, all tailored to the holistic development of multilingual learners of English (MLEs). This move is harmonious with the global shift toward an education that is not exclusively cognitive but is enriched by attending to the social and emotional facets of learners. Such an approach is instrumental in preparing individuals who are academically adept and equally equipped with the resilience, empathy, and competence needed to navigate a complex, globalized world (Elias et al., 1997). The unification of these elements signifies more than a theoretical alignment; it represents a transformative step in ELT. Echoing the sentiments of the affective or emotional turn (White, 2018), it underscores the imperative of an enriched, multidimensional perspective of learning. In this enhanced paradigm, English language education becomes intrinsically intertwined with the broader educational, social, and emotional landscapes. It ensures that learning is not an isolated cognitive journey but a holistic experience that nurtures learners, teachers, and the community at large, fostering a learning environment where academic excellence and human flourishing are mutual, complementary outcomes.

What Social-Emotional Learning Is and Is Not

As we venture deeper into the rich landscape of SEL within our English language classrooms, it becomes essential to have a crystal-clear understanding of what SEL genuinely encompasses as well as what it does not. We are all on this journey together, and clarifying these aspects ensures that we are all on the same page and can make the most out of integrating SEL into our teaching practices. In the spirit of collaboration and clarity, we have put together a table (Table 1) that outlines common misconceptions and myths about what SEL is and what it is not. Our hope is that Table 1 can serve as a practical tool aimed at enhancing our collective understanding and ensuring that when we talk about SEL, we are aligned in our perspectives and approaches.

In addition to Table 1, we would like to share with you an example of what SEL looks like in the classroom. In the boxes below, we share examples of what ELT looks like without SEL, and then we provide the same example and activity with SEL integration. Our hope is that these examples will provide more clarity into how SEL can be seamlessly integrated into ELT practices, transforming not just the learning environment but also the interpersonal dynamics and personal development trajectories of both students and teachers. We believe that demonstrating these contrasts in a practical classroom scenario will offer insights into the tangible differences and enhanced outcomes that arise when SEL is thoughtfully woven into ELT. These examples are meant to illustrate the shift from a traditional, cognitive-centered approach to one that embraces the holistic development of each student, fostering a learning atmosphere where academic and social-emotional growth occur in tandem. We invite you

Table 1 What SEL Is, and What It Is Not

SEL Is	SEL Is Not
A holistic approach to learning	An academic program
Focused on developing emotional intelligence	Ignoring cognitive and academic development
About developing skills like empathy, self-regulation, and communication	Focused solely on traditional educational metrics
Integrative, involving schools, families, and communities	Restricted to classroom learning environments
Evidence-based and research-supported	A trendy buzzword without empirical backing
Tailored to fit diverse learning environments and cultural contexts	A one-size-fits-all solution
Aimed at fostering safe, caring, and participatory school climates	Limiting or restrictive to students' emotional expressions
Enhancing both individual and collective well-being	Solely centered on individual student outcomes
A lifelong learning process	A curriculum with an end point
Empowering students to be responsible and ethical citizens	Detached from real-world applications and ethics

to explore and reflect upon these scenarios, considering the potential implications and transformative effects of integrating SEL into your own teaching
practices and classroom environments.

ELT WITHOUT SEL

In the ELT classroom, lessons are often characterized by a focus on the
cognitive acquisition of language skills, with little attention given to
the social and emotional contexts in which language is embedded and
used. The learning environment is more about transferring knowledge

than fostering a deeper holistic understanding of the language in real-life contexts.

For instance, imagine a lesson where the teacher introduces new vocabulary related to emotions. The teacher provides students with a list of emotion words and definitions and perhaps pictures to match. Each student receives a worksheet and works silently, independently drawing lines to connect words with their meanings. The atmosphere is calm, but interaction among students is minimal.

The teacher, attentive and focused, walks around, monitoring the students' progress. After all, the goal is accuracy—ensuring that each word is matched correctly. Once completed, answers are reviewed collectively, corrections are made, and almost immediately the class transitions to a new topic, perhaps a grammar lesson. While the students have learned new words, the rich and nuanced social and emotional contexts these words exist within remain unexplored. The opportunity to connect these words to students' lives, to explore their meanings in depth, and to foster a shared learning experience is missed. The lesson, though successful in conveying the definitions and building students' vocabulary, does not delve into the lived experiences and emotions these words can evoke.

ELT WITH SEL

In an SEL-integrated ELT classroom, the learning atmosphere is palpably different. Here, language learning is not just an intellectual exercise but also a holistic experience, weaving together cognitive, emotional, and social elements. The classroom is a dynamic space where students do not just learn about the language but also engage with it, connecting new vocabulary and concepts to their own lives and emotions.

Take, for instance, a lesson on emotion vocabulary in this enriched environment. The teacher introduces emotion words, but instead of a straightforward matching exercise, students are encouraged to dive deeper. They explore not just the definitions but the feelings, contexts, and personal experiences associated with these words. Each student receives a flashcard with an emotion word, sparking a journey into personal reflection and shared storytelling.

The classroom buzzes with energy as students pair up, sharing personal stories and experiences linked to their assigned emotion words. It is a vibrant dance of language learning intertwined with social interaction and emotional expression. The teacher facilitates this process, weaving through the pairs, engaging in conversations, and encouraging deeper reflection and sharing.

After sharing, pairs join other pairs, broadening the discussion and adding layers of complexity and richness to the understanding of these emotional words. They are not just words on paper anymore; they are lived experiences, shared narratives, and emotional connections. The vocabulary is brought to life, imbued with personal and shared meanings, connecting students to the language and to each other in profound ways. This immersive approach does not just teach students new words; it invites them into a shared journey of exploration, connection, and understanding, fostering a learning environment where language acquisition and social-emotional development flourish hand in hand. It is not just the interactivity of this lesson that makes it more engaging but also the emphasis on giving students opportunities to identify and share their own emotions with others.

Figure 1, contrasting the cold, impersonal environment without SEL to the warm, engaging atmosphere with SEL, effectively communicates the significant impact of integrating SEL in ELT. The stark differences in color, environment, and activities vividly illustrate the transformative power of SEL. Each side of this visual, accompanied by specific descriptions of classroom practices, serves as a testimony to how SEL breathes life, warmth, and connection into the learning experience, transforming the classroom from an arid space of mere information transfer to a vibrant community of holistic growth and learning.

Essential Terminology to Know

As we delve deeper into SEL in ELT, and into our book, we find it paramount to establish a common language. For this reason, in this section, we introduce and define key terms and concepts integral to understanding and effectively implementing SEL in the ELT context. By familiarizing ourselves with these terms, we lay a foundation for meaningful discourse, shared understanding, and effective practices throughout this monograph. We also provide Figure 2

ENGLISH LANGUAGE TEACHING WITH SEL

THE TEACHER IS AMONG THE STUDENTS, FACILITATING DISCUSSIONS. THEIR POSTURE OPEN AND INVITING.

STUDENTS ARE IN GROUPS, ACTIVELY PARTICIPATING. THEIR EXPRESSIONS INDICATE CURIOSITY, AND ENJOYMENT.

VARIOUS SEATING ARRANGEMENTS AND COZY CORNERS EXIST, PROMOTING INCLUSIVITY AND COMMUNITY.

THE BOARD DISPLAYS NOT ONLY ACADEMIC CONTENT BUT ALSO AFFIRMATIONS; STUDENTS' WORKS, AND PROMPTS THAT ENCOURAGE EMOTIONAL EXPRESSION AND SOCIAL INTERACTION.

EVALUATIONS ARE HOLISTIC, EVALUATING ACADEMIC, EMOTIONAL, AND SOCIAL GROWTH TO PROVIDE A COMPREHENSIVE VIEW OF STUDENT DEVELOPMENT.

ENGLISH LANGUAGE TEACHING WITHOUT SEL

THE TEACHER STANDS AT THE FRONT, DELIVERING A LECTURE. THERE IS A CLEAR DIVIDE BETWEEN THE TEACHER AND THE STUDENTS.

STUDENTS ARE SEATED IN ROWS, PASSIVELY RECEIVING INFORMATION. THEIR FACIAL EXPRESSIONS INDICATE A LACK OF ENGAGEMENT OR CONNECTION.

THE CLASSROOM LAYOUT IS UNIFORM AND STARK, LACKING ELEMENTS THAT PROMOTE WARMTH OR COMMUNITY.

THE BOARD DISPLAYS STRICTLY ACADEMIC CONTENT, FOCUSING SOLELY ON LANGUAGE STRUCTURE AND RULES.

STUDENTS ARE EVALUATED SOLELY BASED ON TEST SCORES AND ACADEMIC ACHIEVEMENTS, NEGLECTING EMOTIONAL AND SOCIAL DEVELOPMENT.

Figure 1: Two Worlds of Learning: The Impact of SEL Integration in ELT

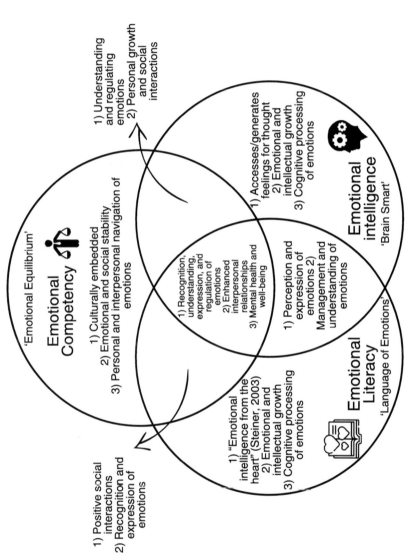

Figure 2: Emotional Competency, Emotional Intelligence, and Emotional Literacy

below to compare and contrast the terms *emotional competency, emotional intelligence,* and *emotional literacy,* which are often misunderstood and used interchangeably, even though they are independent terms.

Social-emotional learning: The process by "which children and adults acquire and apply competencies to recognize and manage emotions, set and achieve positive goals, appreciate the perspectives of others, establish and maintain supportive relationships, make responsible decisions, and handle personal and interpersonal situations constructively" (Osher et al., 2016, p. 645).

Emotional competency: A multifaceted and culturally embedded concept encompassing the skills and abilities to perceive, understand, express, and regulate emotions effectively, contributing to social and emotional stability and adaptability. It refers to one's capacity to navigate emotional experiences, both personally and interpersonally, in a healthy and constructive manner (Saarni, 1999).

Emotional intelligence: The ability to "perceive accurately, appraise, and express emotion; the ability to access and/or generate feelings when they facilitate thought; the ability to understand emotion and emotional knowledge; and the ability to regulate emotions to promote emotional and intellectual growth" (Mayer & Salovey, 1997, p. 10).

Emotional literacy: The ability to recognize, understand, express, and manage one's own emotions and the emotions of others, serving as a foundation for empathetic and effective social interactions. Emotional literacy supports mental health, positive relationships, and social success. This term is commonly confused with the term *emotional intelligence.* According to Steiner, the difference between emotional intelligence and emotional literacy is that "emotional literacy is emotional intelligence from the heart" (2003, p. 32).

Final Thoughts

We end Chapter 1 by extending a heartfelt invitation for you, our fellow educators and readers, to pause and reflect. As language teachers, we know that the journey through the landscapes of our classrooms is one marked by continuous learning, adaptation, and growth. Each day, as we step into these dynamic spaces, we are not just teaching English—we are shaping lives, molding perspectives, and building futures. Imagine, for a moment, a classroom where language learning intertwines seamlessly with the nurturing of emotional intelligence, the cultivation of emotional literacy, and the flowering of emotional competence. This merging of linguistic and social-emotional development opens up an expansive new frontier in our teaching journey.

Now, with that vision in mind, think about your teaching practices, the methodologies you hold dear, and the strategies you apply with precision and care. Perhaps you are already infusing SEL into your practice. Perhaps there are opportunities for further integration of SEL in your pedagogy. And perhaps this is a new concept for you. Wherever you are in your journey of incorporating SEL in your practice, we invite you to join us. Envisage your classroom through the lens of SEL, where every lesson, interaction, and evaluation is not just a step toward linguistic proficiency but a leap toward holistic human development. By infusing SEL into our practice, every conversation, piece of feedback, and expression of understanding can be a touchstone for social and emotional growth. The words we choose, the activities we design, and the environments we create are fertile grounds where the seeds of SEL can be sown. Through this ongoing practice, we begin to realize that, more than a strategy or teaching approach, SEL can also become our pedagogy.

We want to invite you to take a step back, look at your classroom with new eyes, and embrace the transformative power of integrating SEL into our ELT practices. Imagine the boundless horizons where our students learn a language while also cultivating the social and emotional skills that will aid them as they navigate through life's intricate tapestry with grace, resilience, and empathy. This is not a distant dream or a theoretical concept; it is a hands-on, heart-centered approach in which each of us has the power to turn our classrooms into gardens of social and emotional learning, blooming with empathy, resilience, and understanding. As you delve deeper into this book, we invite you to look at your teaching practice with fresh eyes and an open heart. Together, we are stepping into a world rich with opportunities where the confluence of language teaching and human development becomes a vibrant dance of transformation, enlightening not just our students but ourselves.

Chapter 2
Why Social-Emotional Learning in Language Teaching?

Introduction

We find ourselves in an unprecedented era. War, hostility, apathy, and violence are reaching alarming levels around the world, while technology simultaneously accelerates at an extraordinary pace (Milanovic, 2023). As technology expands and reshapes every part of our reality, from the economy to politics and health, our social spaces, notably education, must evolve in tandem. Formal education, echoing the broader societal context, has traditionally morphed in response to prevailing challenges, recalibrating its methodologies and priorities. In these times, schools face the daunting task of addressing the dual challenges presented by escalating instability and rapid technological growth. This interplay between unrest and technology is multifaceted. While technology offers the prospects of connectivity, accessibility, and democratization of knowledge (Mishra, 2015), it also presents challenges. There are instances where technology exacerbates divisions, spreads hate, or even foments violence (Limone & Toto, 2022). This dual nature of technology urges educators to rethink teaching paradigms, and in doing so, reconsider the broader dimensions of literacy.[1]

Literacy, as Street (1984) conceptualized, goes beyond mere reading and writing, encompassing cultural practices deeply rooted in societal contexts. These practices mirror the intricate ways in which societies communicate, perceive, and relate. With technology's rapid advances, the boundaries of literacy have expanded to include digital competencies, emphasizing the intertwined nature of cognitive and emotional processes. However, the essence of literacy—its human and social core—remains steadfast. In today's world, inhumanity and misunderstandings proliferate, underlining the importance of effective communication and emotional understanding. This necessitates

---

1. We understand and recognize Brian Street's (1984) preference for *literacies* instead of *literacy*. We agree with Brian Street's definition and conceptualization. However, for uniformity, we spell the construct as *literacy* throughout this manuscript.

an exploration into a specific dimension of literacy—emotional literacy, which is described as the ability to recognize, understand, and express one's emotions and to interpret those of others (Steiner & Perry, 1997). As the lines between the digital and physical worlds blur, with conflict increasing on both fronts, emotional literacy becomes paramount in helping individuals process the traumatic effects of violence, understand its roots, and develop empathy (Gottfredson & Becker, 2023).

Navigating this era necessitates a holistic approach to literacy that merges technical prowess with emotional depth. Students grapple not just with the mechanics of language and technology but also with their identities, relationships, and roles within tumultuous contexts. This intricate weave of modern forms of literacy underlines the paramount importance of emotional intelligence (see Goleman, 2005), particularly given AI's limitations in replicating human nuances. As Beck & Libert (2017) astutely observed, the technological ascent accentuates the indispensable nature of genuine human interaction, understanding, and creativity. This is where SEL finds its footing and proves itself vital in the education of our future generation. By infusing SEL into educational curricula, we equip children and adults with the tools to traverse the intricate terrains of both the digital realm and the emotional landscapes that shape our physical and virtual worlds (Chatterjee Singh & Duraiappah, 2020). In this chapter, we delve into the rich landscape of literacy, especially emotional literacy, unraveling its intersections with language acquisition. Further, we establish the symbiotic relationship between emotional literacy and language learning, highlighting the empirical and theoretical underpinnings that endorse their integration for enriched learning experiences.

Literacy: A Brief Overview

Initially, literacy was often narrowly defined as the ability to read and write. This basic conception stemmed from the practical needs of societies, where being literate simply meant having the skills to sign one's name or to read (Langer, 2014). Simultaneously, in pre-colonial and colonial times, literacy was used as a tool for enslavement and social inequality, as it was often reserved for those in positions of power and prestige (Tierney & Pearson, 2021). As societies advanced, so did the expectations associated with being literate and with having access to literacy. The introduction of print media and its widespread accessibility in the Renaissance period, for example, brought about a shift where literacy began to encompass understanding and interpretation of printed materials (Eisenstein, 1980) and became more accessible to the masses.

In the twentieth century, with the rise of diverse media and increased global connectivity, literacy expanded to incorporate the capacity to interpret and critically evaluate information from various sources, including radio, television, and, later, the internet (Livingstone, 2004). This broader conceptualization, often termed "media literacy," recognized that in an age of information overload, mere reading and writing skills were insufficient. Around this time, Street (1984) introduced the idea of "ideological" and "autonomous" models of literacy. The autonomous model views literacy as a neutral skill, whereas the ideological model perceives literacy practices as deeply embedded within specific social contexts and cultural practices. This recognition shifted the discourse from viewing literacy as a standalone skill to understanding it within the intricate interplay of culture, power, and social practices.

The digital revolution of the twenty-first century further transformed the concept of literacy. Digital literacy, a term popularized in academic and policy discourses, refers to an individual's ability to find, evaluate, and communicate information using digital platforms (Gilster, 1997). This form of literacy not only involves technical proficiency but also emphasizes critical thinking and ethical behavior in digital environments (Hobbs, 2010). Today, literacy is understood as a multifaceted entity that encompasses traditional reading and writing skills but extends to the ability to interpret, understand, and create content and knowledge across various mediums and platforms (Cope & Kalantzis, 2000). As we journey through the various phases of literacy's evolution, it is beneficial to visualize the transformation. Illustrating the broad spectrum of literacy from its nascent stages to its modern manifestations, Figure 3 captures the different types of literacy (in a non-exhaustive list) pertinent to today's interconnected world.

From its rudimentary conception to its multifaceted understanding today, literacy has been inextricably intertwined with the zeitgeist of its era (Tierney & Pearson, 2021). Its dynamic evolution reflects the changing demands and complexities of society. While the spectrum of literacy has expanded to encompass a myriad of skills, certain facets remain undervalued. For example, although most of the types of literacy shown in Figure 3 receive recognition and have been integrated into academic spaces, emotional literacy visibly remains marginalized, especially in language education (Pentón Herrera & Martínez-Alba, 2022). This is an oversight that warrants attention in our field, especially when considering the critical twenty-first-century skills identified as essential for future success.

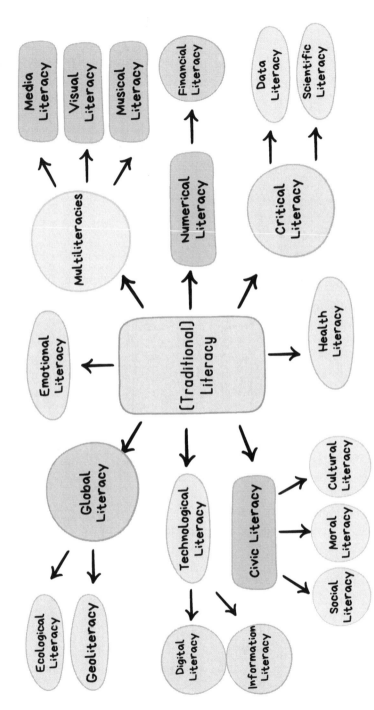

Figure 3: Different Types of Literacy in Today's Society

The anticipated foundational skills necessary for success in 2030 include literacy, numeracy, and digital and information communication technology (ICT). In addition, the core transferable skills comprise "problem-solving, critical thinking, and communication while additional skills included analysis, creativity, collaboration, leadership and entrepreneurship" (Aker et al., 2018, p. 167)—all SEL competencies. Regrettably, the predominant test-driven notion of literacy in contemporary education often overlooks these core SEL skills. Such a limited perspective neglects the fluid nature of literacy and the diverse capacities students inherently possess. With societal progression, it is essential for our educational curricula to evolve, both to celebrate the diverse cultural and academic backgrounds of our students and to prepare them for a swiftly changing world.

Emotional Literacy

As we go deeper into our conversation, we find it necessary to define emotional literacy, clarifying elements of it that are sometimes misunderstood. Emotional literacy is defined as the skill to comprehend our own feelings, the aptitude to tune in to and resonate with others' emotions, and the capability to effectively convey emotions. "To be an emotionally literate person is to be able to handle emotions in a way that improves your personal power . . . and the quality of life around you" (Steiner & Perry, 1997, p. 11). Numerous academic discussions underscore the pivotal role of emotional literacy in influencing cognitive processes, learning outcomes, and interpersonal relationships (e.g., Malkoç & Zeynep, 2020; Srikanth & Sonawat, 2012). Scholars and educators alike have spotlighted how the successful development of emotional literacy can serve as a bedrock for critical thinking, decision-making, and conflict resolution (Ladd, 2003; Pelin, 2021). Studies further illuminate its potential to enhance student engagement, foster a positive learning environment, and bolster resilience in challenging situations (Bezzina & Camilleri, 2021; Sotiriadis & Galanakis, 2022). By weaving emotional literacy into the tapestry of academic discourse, we, English teachers, not only recognize its significance but also pave the way for holistic educational practices that value both the cognitive and emotional dimensions of learning (Waterhouse, 2019).

In contemporary academic discussions, *emotional literacy* is often confused with, or used interchangeably with, the term *emotional intelligence*; however, they represent distinct concepts. Emotional literacy, which predates emotional intelligence, encompasses the capacity to identify, comprehend, and aptly convey the emotions of oneself and of others. It is frequently regarded as a core aspect of emotional intelligence, underlining the significance of an effective emotional vocabulary for genuine communication. Conversely, emotional intelligence delves deeper into an individual's inherent ability to manage emotions, spur self-motivation, discern emotions in others, and cultivate fruitful relationships, as delineated by Goleman (2005). To distinguish, Alemdar & Anılan (2020) note that while emotional intelligence denotes a natural propensity to engage with emotions, emotional literacy provides a range of abilities that, when taught and honed, foster proficient emotional communication. In our view, differentiating between emotional literacy and emotional intelligence is paramount for educators and curriculum developers. A clear distinction allows for more tailored interventions, ensuring that students receive the support that they need. By understanding the nuances between these concepts, educators can design curricula that not only bolster students' emotional vocabulary (i.e., emotional literacy) but also enhance their inherent capabilities to manage and engage with emotions (i.e., emotional intelligence).

Ultimately, both emotional literacy and emotional intelligence serve as pillars supporting the overarching structure of emotional health. Recognizing and valuing these capacities in educational settings not only enriches the academic experience but also contributes profoundly to nurturing individuals who are well equipped for the emotional complexities of modern life. Thus, emphasizing emotional development in our curricula can significantly elevate the overall well-being of our students, preparing them for academic and life challenges. In Figure 4, we share a comparison between emotional literacy and emotional intelligence, alongside some considerations for teaching these skills in our language classrooms. Also, in Appendix 1, we share more details about the considerations for teaching these skills.

Emotional Development and Language Learning

The nexus between emotional development and language acquisition is profound and multidimensional. Embracing the broader umbrella of emotional development, which includes both emotional literacy and emotional intelligence, allows us to examine the deep intertwining of emotions with the cognitive processes that are integral to language learning.

Emotional literacy greatly influences language learners' receptivity to new linguistic information. As students grapple with the challenges of language acquisition, their emotional experiences either bolster or hinder

EMOTIONAL LITERACY

EMOTIONAL INTELLIGENCE

DIFFERENCES

Understanding the fundamental aspects of emotions and how they are expressed, including:
- Recognizing and naming one's own emotions
- Reading and interpreting emotional expressions of others
- Understanding the difference between feelings and actions
- Effective verbal communication of one's emotions

Going beyond mere recognition. Delving into the regulation and application of emotions, including:
- Self-motivation and persistence
- Managing unsettling emotions calmly and effectively
- Recognizing emotions in others and responding empathetically
- Handling interpersonal relationships judiciously and empathetically

SIMILARITIES

Certain traits form the core of both emotional literacy and intelligence, serving as a bridge between recognition and management of emotions. These include:
- Understanding emotions
- Interpersonal emotional recognition
- Empathizing with others
- Regulating emotions
- Emotional self-awareness

CONSIDERATIONS

Teaching emotional skills, be it literacy or intelligence, requires a thoughtful approach that recognizes the diverse emotional needs and backgrounds of students. When integrating these teachings into classrooms, especially language classrooms, educators might consider:
- Tailored activities
- Safe environments
- Storytelling
- Interactive games
- Reflection time
- Modeling

Figure 4: Emotional Literacy and Emotional Intelligence

their cognitive engagement (Namaziandost et al., 2023; Wang et al., 2023). Desired emotional states can heighten attentiveness, receptivity, and motivation, setting the stage for optimal language absorption. Conversely, when faced with undesired emotions like frustration or anxiety, learners might find themselves disengaged or disheartened, stalling their language development journey (MacIntyre et al., 2019). Equally vital is emotional intelligence, which fosters meaningful interpersonal interactions. Within the language classroom, emotional intelligence aids in understanding and navigating the intricate tapestry of human communication beyond mere lexical or grammatical comprehension (Goleman, 1998; Soodmand Afshar & Rahimi, 2016). An emotionally intelligent learner can better discern nuances in tone, mood, or context, making their linguistic interactions richer and more authentic.

The integration of emotional development into language learning is further emphasized when considering second language acquisition, where students often confront a gamut of emotions. Delving into a new linguistic system can evoke feelings ranging from exhilaration and curiosity to trepidation and self-doubt. When educators equip learners with tools and strategies grounded in emotional development, they facilitate a more nurturing and effective learning environment. This understanding resonates with the affective filter hypothesis proposed by Krashen (1982), suggesting that emotional barriers can obstruct language input processing. Hence, cultivating an emotionally supportive environment becomes imperative to ensuring optimal language acquisition and fostering students' confidence and resilience in the face of linguistic challenges.

Furthermore, as Alemdar & Anılan (2020) elucidate, while emotional intelligence signifies a natural aptitude to engage with emotions, emotional literacy offers a tool kit that, once cultivated, ensures effective emotional communication. This distinction is paramount for educators. By understanding the interplay between these facets of emotional development, curricula can be designed not only to enhance students' emotional vocabulary but also to bolster their inherent capabilities to navigate emotional landscapes in language learning. In summary, emotional development, encompassing both emotional literacy and emotional intelligence, serves as a cornerstone in the edifice of comprehensive language education. Recognizing its centrality and integrating it systematically into curricula can significantly elevate students' linguistic proficiencies while also preparing them for the intricate emotional complexities of real-world communication.

Affective Communicative Competence and SEL

I have learned that people will forget what you said, people will forget what you did, but people will never forget how you made them feel.
                                                                    — *Maya Angelou*

Maya Angelou's words serve as a poignant reminder of the intricate interplay between language and emotion. They emphasize that communication is not merely about the transfer of information or the precise articulation of thoughts. Instead, it is fundamentally about evoking and acknowledging feelings—making someone feel seen, heard, and understood. In the domain of language teaching, this symbiotic relationship between words and emotions epitomizes emotional literacy.

To truly understand and harness the power of language, students must venture beyond vocabulary and grammar. They must be adept at discerning the subtle emotional undertones of words, understanding the feelings behind spoken phrases, and conveying their own emotions articulately. This intricate skill set, which binds emotions tightly with language, culminates in what we term and propose as *affective communicative competence*. Building on the work of Hymes (1972) on communicative competence, we define the term *affective communicative competence* as an individual's ability to recognize, understand, and convey emotions and feelings within the context of communication. It encompasses the skills to interpret and produce language that accurately reflects emotional nuances as well as the capability to respond empathetically and appropriately to the emotional content in the communication of others. This form of competence goes beyond the mere structural and functional aspects of language, emphasizing the importance of emotional resonance and understanding in authentic communication.

In our view, affective communicative competence is not just an academic concept—it is a vital life skill, central to every facet of human interaction. As we navigate an increasingly globalized world, where cross-cultural exchanges are commonplace, the need to convey and comprehend emotions across language barriers becomes even more pronounced. It is about more than understanding words; it is about feeling the weight and intent behind them, reading between the lines, and grasping the emotions of speakers from diverse cultural backgrounds (Mesquita, 2022). The ability to convey not just content, but also emotion and intent, is paramount. Affective communicative competence demands a deep integration of affective elements in language learning, ensuring that learners can express and interpret emotions authentically and accurately. Emotional literacy, as a pillar of SEL, plays an instrumental role in cultivating this affective communicative competence. It takes learners beyond syntax and semantics, immersing them in the rich emotional tapestry of human communication, where feelings and words dance in tandem.

While the cultivation of affective communicative competence is crucial for nuanced linguistic interactions, it is also deeply rooted in fulfilling basic human emotional needs. The essence of effective communication is not just in the words we say but in the underlying emotions that drive and shape those words. Our language learners' journeys are influenced by a myriad of emotional experiences, stemming from both innate human needs and their individual encounters with language (Pentón Herrera & Martínez-Alba, 2021). Addressing these foundational emotional needs becomes paramount not just for individual well-being but also for creating an environment conducive to authentic, empathetic communication. Recognizing and addressing these needs elevates the learning experience from merely acquiring linguistic skills to genuinely connecting with others. According to Salcedo (2018, pp. 112–113), all humans, regardless of our differences, have eight basic social-emotional needs. The intensity of these eight basic needs may vary at different times of our lives and depend on our beliefs and personalities, but they are present at varying levels. They are:

1. **To be safe and secure.** Individuals need to feel safe both physically and mentally to effectively develop and prosper.
2. **To be loved and have a sense of self-worth.** As humans, we need to feel worthy of love and feel like someone cares for us and loves us.
3. **To be acknowledged and understood.** Individuals have the need to feel acknowledged, heard, and understood by those around them.
4. **To have a sense of control and predictability.** Children and adults need to feel like we are in control of our lives and actions. For this reason, routines, traditions, and rituals are important because they help create a sense of predictability and stability in our daily lives.
5. **To recognize and be able to regulate our emotions.** Emotions are ever-present, and they often affect our behavior even before we understand what they are. Our social-emotional development depends on our ability to recognize and regulate our emotions, as opposed to letting them control us and our behavior.
6. **To feel independent and competent.** Feeling independent and competent promotes vital human qualities such as confidence, self-esteem, self-trust, motivation, and creativity.

7. **To be engaged in stimulating pursuits.** Our brains require stimulation to survive and thrive. Individuals need safe, engaging spaces where they can freely explore and engage in solutions to problems of interest.

8. **To enjoy relationships and have a sense of belonging.** Human beings are, by design, social creatures. We need to feel like we belong and are valued in our social circles and communities and that we have meaningful social relationships with others.

While Salcedo's eight foundational emotional needs provide a comprehensive understanding of individual human necessities, they also lay the groundwork for a broader discourse on the impact and role of SEL in our classrooms. Each of these needs, from the desire for security to the longing for a sense of belonging, underscores the importance of equipping learners with the skills and competencies to navigate a complex world of emotions and relationships. For us, incorporating SEL into our practice, philosophy, and environment is the solution and vehicle to accomplishing such tasks because, in our view, emotional development is not just about individual well-being; it is about shaping the very fabric of our learning communities and, by extension, the wider world. With this perspective in mind, we would like to propose three main reasons why we should incorporate SEL in language teaching:

First, **SEL as a practice illuminates the pathway to meeting students' social-emotional needs**. It equips educators with direct actions and methods that are tailored to the unique challenges and opportunities presented by language education. When we, educators, integrate SEL practices into our pedagogy, we are not just teaching language—we are fostering spaces where students can feel safe, valued, and emotionally attuned. Through SEL, we can employ strategies that allow learners to process their emotions, better understand those of others, and express themselves with clarity and empathy (see Pentón Herrera 2024). As Osher et al. (2016) have elucidated, SEL interventions can lead to significant improvements in students' social behaviors, reduced emotional stress, and enhanced academic performance.

Second, **SEL as a pedagogy emphasizes its foundational role in shaping the very beliefs and principles that drive language education**. The philosophical underpinnings of SEL champion the holistic development of students, viewing them not just as language learners but as whole individuals with a diverse range of emotions, experiences, and aspirations. By incorporating SEL into the pedagogical framework, educators acknowledge that true learning is an amalgamation of cognitive, affective, and sociocultural processes. As Elias et al. (1997) posited, SEL-based pedagogy nurtures the heart alongside the mind, creating a more enriched, balanced, and holistic educational experience for learners and educators alike.

Lastly, **SEL as an ecosystem presents a broader vision where individual practices and pedagogical beliefs coalesce to shape thriving communities and a harmonious world**. In this perspective, classrooms are not isolated entities but are deeply interconnected with the wider community and world. The ripple effects of SEL reverberate beyond the walls of educational institutions, influencing families, communities, and societies at large. By nurturing emotionally literate and communicatively competent individuals, educators are, in essence, cultivating ambassadors of empathy, understanding, and positive change for the global community. SEL's ecosystemic impact has the potential to foster healthier interpersonal relationships, more cohesive communities, and a world where diverse individuals can communicate and collaborate harmoniously (Elias et al., 1997; Pentón Herrera, 2024; Pentón Herrera & McNair, 2021).

Final Thoughts

In this chapter, we have introduced the concepts of emotional literacy and emotional intelligence, highlighting their relationship with language learning. In addition, we proposed and defined affective communicative competence as a vital SEL skill to include in our English language classrooms.

As we end this chapter, we would like to close with a scenario of what one might see upon entering into a space that centers SEL in their practice and instruction. Visualize with us:

> We walk into first-grade English as an additional language (EAL) classroom, where the curriculum is focused on mathematics content. Here, we see the students working on learning the English names for shapes (e.g., circle, square, etc.). After the teacher has guided students in recognizing the different names of shapes and their properties, they ask students to form groups. Once in their groups, the teacher prompts students to share a triangle of feelings that each has at that moment. The students are encouraged to just share and listen as each member

names three feelings they are experiencing. When students are done sharing, the teacher explains that it is normal to have many different feelings in one day. Then, the teacher encourages students to identify a pentagon of feelings that they all have had at some point that week. The teacher passes out a paper with five pentagons on it, each with the sentence frame: When _____ happened, I felt _____. To conclude the lesson, the teacher reviews the different names of shapes and their properties with the students, and has them do a box breathing exercise: breathing in for four counts, holding their breath for four counts, breathing out for four counts, and holding their breath for four counts (if students are uncomfortable holding their breath, they may just practice breathing in for four counts and out for four counts). They repeat four times, and the lesson ends.

In this scenario, we see the teacher infusing SEL into a mathematics lesson. Students demonstrate their understanding of mathematical concepts and language through their work and communication. They are given time to identify and share their emotions as well as time to practice listening to others and identifying similarities of feelings among group members. While students could certainly learn their shapes by matching shapes and definitions on a worksheet and drawing and labeling shapes on their papers, the lesson in the scenario above centers the emotions of students, fostering not only an understanding of self but also a commitment to fostering understanding of others.

Chapter 3
How to Include Social-Emotional Learning in Language Teaching

Introduction

Maria, a curious student whose recent arrival in the country has been marked by a cacophony of challenges, sits quietly in a bustling middle school English language classroom while her classmates work very diligently on an activity assigned by Mr. Santana, the English teacher. Mr. Santana, who is very empathetic to the emotional currents of his classroom, notices Maria's withdrawn demeanor as the other classmates continue to delve into a lesson on descriptive adjectives.

Today, the class is exploring the language of emotions—words that paint the internal landscape of characters in stories and, perhaps, of the students themselves. Mr. Santana, who has recently identified a need for healthy emotional expression, sees an opportunity through this activity not just to teach English but to tend to the social and emotional landscape of his students.

As the students list out adjectives on the whiteboard, Mr. Santana observes Maria's hesitation to participate. When the group activity shifts to writing personal narratives using the descriptive words collected on the whiteboard, Maria's pencil barely touches the paper. Mr. Santana realizes that for Maria, and indeed for all his students, the mastery of language is intertwined with their emotional expression and confidence.

With a gentle pivot, Mr. Santana decides to weave SEL into the fabric of his lesson. He pauses the writing task and gathers the class into a circle. Here, in a space that feels more intimate and less structured than traditional rows of desks, he begins a conversation about the emotional dimensions of language.

"Language is more than words and rules," Mr. Santana says. "It's the bridge between our inner worlds and the outer world. It's how we share who we are, how we feel, and what matters to us."

He introduces a simple yet profound SEL activity: each student is to share a word that describes their current feeling and, if they feel comfortable, a little about why they feel that way. As the circle of sharing moves along, words like "anxious," "excited," "confused," and "hopeful" echo in the space. When it's Maria's turn, she hesitates, but the supportive nods from her peers draw out a soft "overwhelmed."

Mr. Santana acknowledges her bravery in sharing and relates it to a character from a story they have been reading, illustrating how emotions can connect personal experiences with learning. By validating her feelings, Mr. Santana is not just teaching English; he's fostering emotional literacy and building a community of empathy.

Mr. Santana then gently guides the students back to their personal narratives, this time with a new prompt: to weave these shared feelings into their stories, allowing characters to come alive with emotional depth.

Mr. Santana's story may resonate with many of us, English teachers, as we often experience similar situations in the classroom where emotions, if left unaddressed or neglected, can affect the academic experiences of our learners and even their motivation to participate and attend our class. Research has shown that emotions play a pivotal role in the process of learning. The intertwining of cognitive and emotional processes is evident in every classroom, as learners bring their intellectual and emotional selves to the learning environment (Arnold & Brown, 1999). Introducing and reviewing the role of emotions in education, Schutz and Pekrun (2007) highlight that some emotions, such as interest and excitement, can enhance learning, while other emotions, like anxiety, may impede it. Recognizing the profound impact of emotions on learning, educators across the globe have begun to prioritize SEL as an integral part of the educational journey (Mok, 2019). Not only does SEL provide a foundation for safer and more beneficial learning environments, but it also strengthens students' relationships with the subject matter, allowing for deeper understanding and engagement (McCormick et al., 2015).

Chapter 3 stands as a testament to this imperative shift in education. Here, we delve into the pragmatic realm, offering you, our dedicated readers and educators, tangible and actionable steps to seamlessly integrate SEL into language teaching practices. Throughout this chapter, we will guide you on a step-by-step journey: from exploring various SEL frameworks and competencies and understanding how to select the ones that best fit your classroom to planning lessons that intertwine language learning with emotional growth and, finally, how to incorporate and assess SEL in your teaching. Our aim is to empower you with the knowledge and tools to create a classroom where both language and emotions flourish side by side, enriching each other in the process. By the end of this chapter, we hope you will be equipped to make SEL a cornerstone of your teaching approach, much like Mr. Santana, thereby ensuring a more holistic learning experience for your students.

SEL SPOTLIGHT: HAPPINESS

One powerful approach to deepen our students' understanding of emotions is by connecting them with their senses. Our senses provide a direct path to evoke and express feelings, making them a valuable tool in SEL. This activity is a fantastic way to explore the multifaceted nature of happiness by engaging each of the five senses. In doing this, students can relate the abstract concept of emotions to concrete sensory experiences, providing a richer context for understanding and expressing their feelings.

Happiness looks like (sight)_____
Happiness sounds like (hearing)_____
Happiness smells like (smell)_____
Happiness tastes like (taste)_____
Happiness feels like (touch)_____

We recommend prompting your students to reflect and complete each sentence. Encourage them to share and discuss their responses. It can lead to enlightening conversations about the diversity of individual experiences and perceptions, reminding us all that while we may all feel happiness, the ways in which we experience it can be wonderfully unique. Other emotions can be used for this activity, and teachers might even prompt students to choose one emotion they are currently feeling or would like to explore more thoroughly as they engage with both language and their senses.

Frameworks, Competencies, and Activities

Before delving deeper, it is crucial to distinguish three terms that, though related, are not interchangeable: frameworks, competencies, and activities. These terms are frequently used in the discourse on SEL, sometimes incorrectly as synonyms, which can lead to confusion.

SEL frameworks are the overarching structures that provide comprehensive models and guidelines for implementing social-emotional learning within educational settings. They lay the groundwork, articulating the essential elements of SEL and outlining how it can be woven into the fabric of educational curricula and culture. Notable examples include the CASEL framework and the Promoting Alternative THinking Strategies (PATHS) framework. In contrast, **SEL competencies** refer to the specific skills and abilities that SEL endeavors to develop in students. These are the targets of SEL instruction, such as emotional intelligence and emotional agility, which are key for students to navigate life effectively. Lastly, **SEL activities** are the tangible exercises and practices employed by educators to foster these competencies in their students. These are hands-on, student-centered, and reflective by nature, aiming to engage students in applying SEL skills in concrete situations. For instance, activities might include writing reflective poetry or participating in cooperative games.

We provide Figure 5 as a way to visually encapsulate these concepts. Here, we present an analogy: *In the world of SEL, frameworks are the ocean, competencies are the clouds, and activities are the rain.* This analogy draws inspiration from the water cycle—a process of continuous movement and transformation. The vast and deep ocean of frameworks is the source. From this source, through the process of "evaporation"—representing, in our view, learning and growth—competencies form like clouds. These then give way to "precipitation," the activities that shower down, enriching students' experiences and eventually flowing back into the ocean, thus informing and refreshing the frameworks.

Pre-Implementation: Starting with the Self

Before diving into the implementation of SEL, it is vital to first embark on a journey of self-reflection. In teaching, much as in life, our beliefs, biases, and experiences shape our approach to imparting knowledge. The intersection of teaching language and SEL is deeply personal and thus requires educators to

In the world of SEL, frameworks represent the ocean, competencies represent the clouds, and activities represent the rain.

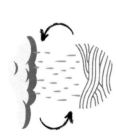

SEL Frameworks

SEL frameworks provide structured models and guidelines for implementing social-emotional learning in educational environments. They offer a foundation for understanding what comprises SEL and how it can be integrated into curricula and school culture.

Examples:
- CASEL Framework
- PATHS Framework

SEL Competencies

SEL competencies are the core skills and abilities that SEL aims to cultivate in students. These include but are not limited to, understanding and managing emotions, setting and achieving positive goals, feeling and showing empathy for others, and making responsible decisions.

Examples:
- Emotional intelligence
- Emotional agility

SEL Activities

SEL activities are practical exercises and practices that educators can implement to develop SEL competencies in students. These activities are interactive, student-centered, and often reflective, designed to engage students in real-life applications of SEL skills.

Examples:
- Writing poetry
- Cooperative games/activities

Figure 5: Frameworks, Competencies, and Activities

introspect and address their underlying ideologies about teaching languages, SEL, and pedagogy in general. The choices, methods, and beliefs of educators impact not only students' academic achievements but also their emotional well-being. It is a well-established fact that self-aware teachers are more effective, not just in imparting knowledge but also in molding character (Žydžiūnaitė & Daugėla, 2020). Thus, before delving into the application of SEL, the journey must begin with a mirror held to oneself.

Below, we share some elements to consider and reflect on before implementing SEL. We hope you find these prompts and questions helpful as you begin to uncover the ideologies guiding your pedagogy.

Personal Reflection

Begin by introspecting on the following:

- Teaching philosophies: Reflect on your core teaching beliefs. What role do you envision for yourself in the classroom? How does this align with SEL? Have there been instances where you revisited and revised these beliefs? If so, what brought about that change?
- Language teaching perspective: Language is not just a means of communication; it is an expression of culture, identity, and emotion. Reflect on your beliefs about teaching a language. Is it merely about grammar and vocabulary, or is it a holistic approach encompassing cultural nuances, emotional expressions, and personal identities? What does this look like in your classroom?
- Implicit biases: All individuals, including educators, have implicit biases. These biases can sometimes influence our teaching methods and interactions with students. It is crucial to recognize and challenge these biases to ensure that the integration of SEL is inclusive and equitable. What biases do you have? What can you do to mitigate these biases in order to create an equitable learning space?

Influences on Pedagogy

Next, consider the influences that shape your pedagogical approach:

- Cultural background: How does your cultural background influence your teaching style? How might it affect your perspective on SEL?

- Professional development and education: Reflect on your formal professional development. Were there particular modules or philosophies that deeply influenced your approach to teaching? How did these teachings address the emotional aspects of learning?
- Experiences: Past experiences, both positive and negative, mold our teaching approach. Consider moments in your teaching career that significantly influenced your pedagogy. How did these moments shape your views on SEL?

SEL and You

Think about your personal relationship with SEL:

- Personal experiences with SEL: Reflect on your experiences with SEL, both as an educator and possibly as a student. How have these experiences shaped your beliefs about the importance of SEL in language teaching?
- Emotional literacy: Gauge your emotional literacy. How comfortably can you recognize, understand, express, and manage your emotions? How does your emotional literacy influence your ability to teach SEL concepts?
- Emotional safety: Create an emotionally safe environment in the classroom, a process that starts with the teacher. Reflect on strategies you currently employ to ensure emotional safety and areas where you can improve.

Moving Forward

After this introspection, consider setting some personal and professional goals. The self-assessment we share above will not only enhance your understanding and delivery of SEL but also foster a deeper, more genuine connection with your students. By aligning your personal and pedagogical beliefs with SEL, you can create a more holistic and empathetic learning environment, much like Mr. Santana. Lastly, we recommend that you revisit this self-assessment periodically, perhaps at the start of every academic term or year. As your understanding of SEL evolves, ensure that your methods remain aligned, cultivating a nurturing and holistic environment for your students.

SEL SPOTLIGHT: SELF-AWARENESS

One of the foundational pillars of SEL is self-awareness, the introspective understanding of one's own emotions, strengths, areas of growth, and drives. Tapping into this dimension can empower students to relate to their innermost feelings, thereby fostering personal growth. Language serves as an effective tool in this exploration, helping students articulate and process their reflections. Consider the following activity to engage students in a deep dive into self-reflection:
  Mirror of Self

  I am happiest when I _____
  Something that challenges me is _____
  A strength I possess is _____
  Something I'm working on improving is _____
  I feel most understood when _____

Prompt your students to complete each sentence sincerely, delving deeply into their thoughts and feelings. Follow up with a discussion session, allowing students to share their reflections. This sharing not only fosters a supportive classroom community but also aids students in recognizing the spectrum of human emotions and experiences. The diverse range of responses will underscore the individuality of each student's journey, emphasizing that while paths may differ, the quest for self-understanding is universal.

Implementing SEL

One of the best features of SEL is how flexible it is: flexible in the approach to teaching, in the way students learn, and in the way students interact and thrive in the classroom (Chandler, 2022). Contrary to popular belief, SEL can take many shapes and forms, and we teachers can choose from a wide variety of resources provided by the school districts (if available), those freely available online, or resources created by ourselves. At the same time, SEL can be included in the classroom through specific activities, like those shared throughout this and other chapters titled "SEL Spotlight," through specific approaches, like those shared in Appendix 2, or by choosing competencies from established SEL frameworks. Whichever option you choose, you should be guided by your students' needs, your contextual demands and allowances, and the goals that you have for yourself and your learners. In this section, we will walk you through a step-by-step process of how to review and choose the SEL framework(s) appropriate for your English classroom.

Getting Started

There are many SEL frameworks that may be drawn on and/or adapted to align with students' needs in a given context. In fact, there are many online resources to help educators identify SEL frameworks that work for their learners. One of the best tools that is freely available is Harvard's EASEL Lab (http://exploresel.gse.harvard.edu/), where you can explore and compare over forty well-established SEL frameworks.

Choosing your SEL Framework(s)

When choosing your SEL framework(s), you may do so by exploring domain focus, discovering framework connections, or identifying related skills. As a point of clarification, the SEL framework(s) might be chosen for a specific lesson, or teachers might desire to use the SEL framework(s) as their SEL guide throughout their entire school year or as part of their pedagogical practices or pedagogy.

For the purpose of this chapter, let's imagine that we are a middle school English teacher who is interested in supporting students' social competence. As such, we would click on the "compare domains" section of the website, and then click on the "social" domain.

After clicking on the "social" domain, all available frameworks on the website are automatically organized from the highest to lowest percentage in terms of having the most social competencies. The top five SEL frameworks that have embedded the most social competencies on Harvard's EASEL Lab website, for example, are the Employability Skills framework (with 45%), the Head Start framework (36%), the EDC Work Ready Now! framework (35%), the CASEL framework (33%), and the K-12 SEL Standards (Anchorage) (30%). For the purpose of this chapter and the example of the middle school teacher, let's choose "Employability Skills" as our SEL framework.

When clicking on the "Employability Skills" framework, we learn that it was created by the U.S. Department of Education (https://cte.ed.gov/initiatives/employability-skills-framework) and that it includes nine main competencies: (1) applied academic skills, (2) interpersonal skills, (3) personal qualities, (4) critical thinking skills, (5) resource management, (6) technology use, (7) information use, (8) communication skills, and (9) systems thinking. Keeping in mind that our middle school teacher is interested in supporting students' social competence, we can choose the competency of interpersonal skills, which includes five sub-competencies: (1) understands teamwork and works with others, (2) responds to customer needs, (3) exercises leadership, (4) negotiates to resolve conflict, and (5) respects individual differences. After reviewing these five sub-competencies, the teacher chooses to focus on *(1) understands teamwork and works with others*, and *(5) respects individual differences.* As an important point of emphasis and clarification, for each class, we recommend that teachers focus on one or two SEL competencies or skills to be effectively integrated and practiced, ensuring depth and meaningful engagement rather than attempting to address too much at once.

Lesson Planning with SEL

Now that the SEL framework and competencies have been identified, we are ready to begin lesson planning. We recommend following Pentón Herrera and Martínez-Alba's SEL lesson plan template (2021, p. 33), which includes:

1) Language Objectives (i.e., reading, writing, listening, speaking)
2) Content Objectives
3) SEL Competencies
4) Materials (i.e., texts, websites, and apps to help meet the objectives)
5) Procedure (items to consider)
   a) integrating SEL into part of the lesson or throughout the lesson
   b) using small groups to help students feel comfortable to talk and share their work with peers
   c) using technology to aid with instruction
   d) including culturally responsive materials/texts
   e) differentiating to meet the needs of different language proficiency levels
6) Assessment (items to consider)
   a) Assessing language and SEL core competencies
   b) differentiating by providing options for assignments and projects when applicable

Example of a Lesson Plan

Following the lesson plan template provided above and the example of a middle school English teacher who is interested in supporting students' social competence and, therefore, chose *understands teamwork and works with others*, and *respects individual differences* as their SEL competencies, we share an example of an SEL lesson plan below. See also Appendix 3 for the full version and all the materials for this lesson plan.

Topic: Building Teamwork and Respecting Differences Through Literature

Language Objectives:

- Students will be able to collaboratively write a short story in small groups.
- Students will be able to present their story orally to the class.

Content Objectives:

- Students will be able to identify and discuss the importance of teamwork in different contexts.
- Students will be able to recognize and appreciate individual differences in their peers' contributions.

SEL Competencies:

- Students will be able to understand teamwork and work with others.
- Students will respect individual differences.
- These two competencies come from the "Employability Skills" framework identified above.

Materials:

- Short stories showcasing teamwork and individual differences
- Paper, pens, and markers for group work
- Presentation tools (e.g., projector, microphone)

Procedure:

- Begin with a warm-up discussion on teamwork using examples from popular culture or students' personal lives.
- Read a short story as a class that exemplifies teamwork and individual differences.
- Discuss the story's themes and the roles of various characters in the group.
- Divide students into small groups and assign each group to collaboratively write a short story emphasizing the values of teamwork and recognizing individual strengths.
- Allow time for each group to present their story to the class.
- Wrap up with a reflection activity on the importance of respecting individual differences and the value each person brings to a team.

Assessment:

- Assess students' collaborative stories for the "integration of teamwork" and "individual differences" themes.
- Observe and evaluate student presentations for clarity, collaboration, and incorporation of lesson objectives.
- Provide options for students to reflect on the lesson, either through a written assignment or oral discussion, to gauge their understanding and application of SEL competencies.

Extensions:

- Creative expression: Invite students to create a visual representation (like a comic strip or poster) of their story, highlighting the elements of teamwork and individual differences.
- Drama extension: Encourage students to convert their written story into a short skit or play, emphasizing nonverbal communication and collaboration during the performance.
- Literary exploration: Ask students to find examples of teamwork and individual differences in books they have read or movies they have watched. They can write a brief report or give a short presentation on their findings.

Differentiation:

- For emerging readers/writers: Provide sentence starters or a story template for students to use when writing their collaborative story. Additionally, allow the use of storytelling cards or visuals to help them structure their story.
- For advanced learners: Challenge them to incorporate specific literary devices into their stories, such as foreshadowing, metaphor, or symbolism. They can also be tasked with identifying these devices in the initial class story read-aloud.
- For visual or kinesthetic learners: Offer the option to create a storyboard, collage, or physical reenactment of their story, highlighting the themes of teamwork and individual differences.
- For auditory learners: Encourage these students to focus on the oral presentation aspect.

SEL SPOTLIGHT: DIVERSITY

Objective: Recognize and celebrate individual strengths within a collaborative effort.
   Materials: Blank puzzle pieces, markers.
   Steps:

1. Individual design: Each student decorates a puzzle piece that represents a personal strength or trait.
2. Team assembly: In groups, students combine pieces, reflecting on how each unique trait contributes to the whole.
3. Discussion: Briefly discuss the importance of individual contributions within teams.

   Tip: Emphasize that every unique strength is essential for effective collaboration, just as each puzzle piece is vital for completing the picture.

Final Thoughts

In the spirit of continuous growth and pedagogical exploration, we offer a closing narrative that mirrors the journey of many educators who are embarking on the path of integrating SEL into their classrooms.

Imagine Ms. Wang, a teacher with a keen interest in SEL but uncertain about its practical application. She stands before her students, ready to dive into a new unit, filled with the desire to enrich her students' learning experience with the dimensions of SEL. Like Mr. Santana, whose story we shared at the beginning of this chapter, Ms. Wang recognizes the potential of SEL to deepen students' engagement and foster a more inclusive learning environment. She recalls the steps outlined in this chapter and decides to take the plunge by visiting the Harvard EASEL Lab website. With a few clicks, she navigates through the wealth of frameworks and finds one that resonates with her teaching objectives. As she integrates SEL into her lesson on descriptive language, Ms. Wang observes an immediate transformation; the students are not only learning about adjectives but are also expressing their feelings more freely and supporting one another's emotional expression.

Ms. Wang's experience exemplifies the seamless integration of SEL into established content and language objectives, illustrating that SEL is not an extraneous component but rather a fundamental aspect of holistic language education. SEL provides the scaffolding for learners to grow not only intellectually but also socially and emotionally within the classroom community. Thus, it is crucial to recognize that SEL is not an isolated set of practices but a vibrant thread woven into the fabric of our educational tapestry. As educators, our role extends beyond imparting knowledge; we are cultivators of a nurturing space where each student can flourish. By incorporating SEL into our pedagogical repertoire, we are not adding more work to our plate; instead, we are enhancing the quality and depth of our teaching, enriching our students' experiences, and facilitating their growth as empathetic, socially aware individuals.

As this chapter comes to a close, let us carry forward the understanding that SEL is an integral part of education. Let us, like Mr. Santana and Ms. Wang, approach SEL with an open heart and mind, ready to integrate these practices into our teaching. By doing so, we are not only shaping more proficient language users but also nurturing future global citizens equipped with the emotional and social competencies necessary to navigate the complexities of our world.

Chapter 4
Social-Emotional Learning and Responsible Well-Being

Introduction

It was a brisk Monday morning when Ms. Ali shuffled through her notes, her mind as scattered as the papers on her desk. Lately, her usual spark for teaching had dimmed, weighed down by a myriad of personal and professional concerns that clung to her like shadows. Across from her, at a desk near the window, sat Raúl, a student whose bright eyes usually held stories waiting to spill out in an enthusiastic manner. Today, though, his gaze was downcast, and his usual eagerness was replaced by an uncharacteristic silence.

The impact of their troubles was silent yet profound. Ms. Ali, grappling with her own wellness, began the lesson with a half-hearted overview of past participles, a topic that usually invited lively mistakes and learning opportunities. Raúl stared blankly at the worksheet, the words blurring before his eyes, his mind clouded by worries from home that made the grammar exercises seem like insurmountable mountains.

"You know, class," Ms. Ali's voice softened, her usual firmness giving way to a gentler tone. "When it comes to tenses, English—like most languages, really—is pretty straightforward. It's all about the 'when' and the 'how.' That's the simple part. But let me tell you, if we're not in the right headspace, if we're not feeling our best, then figuring out tenses becomes really tricky. It's like trying to make sense of a story with the pages all jumbled up."

The students exchanged puzzled glances, unused to their teacher's metaphorical musings. Raúl, too, looked up, with a confused expression on his face, which momentarily displaced his personal distress.

Ms. Ali sighed, setting aside her lesson plan with resignation. "Let's be honest here," she said, leaning against her desk. "How can we learn about a language when we're struggling to keep our heads above water?

How am I supposed to teach, and how can you all learn, if we're distracted, if we're weighed down by our own worries?"

Raúl raised his hand, emboldened by his teacher's vulnerability. "Ms. Ali," he said. "When my thoughts are racing, the English words don't flow. They just bump into each other."

Ms. Ali nodded. "Exactly, Raúl. And it's the same for me—when my mind is racing with a million things, my words come out all tangled. It's like trying to piece together a puzzle when the pieces are scattered everywhere. I probably don't make much sense when I am physically teaching, but my mind is elsewhere."

The room was quiet, a communal acknowledgment of shared struggle. Ms. Ali took a deep breath. "So, what if we start today with something different? What if we talk about what's making our heads noisy? Maybe, just maybe, if we lighten that load, we can all feel and learn a little better."

That day, the English lesson was unconventional. There were no drills or memorizations. Instead, there was dialogue—a shared exploration of emotions, a collective unpacking of burdens. And in that conversational exchange, Ms. Ali and her students—especially Raúl— found a bridge back to learning, one built not just on grammatical structures but on the foundational stones of understanding and empathy.

The stories of Ms. Ali and Raúl are representative of the increasing and multifaceted challenges that teachers and students face in the English language classroom on a daily basis. As a field, we have grown to acknowledge and understand that the well-being of both teachers and students plays a pivotal role in the dynamics of English language education. We have come to understand that teachers' emotional states significantly influence their teaching behaviors and effectiveness and, consequently, students' learning experiences and success (Cheng et al., 2022; Pentón Herrera et al., 2023a). Among teachers, low well-being is often caused by stress and burnout, which can lead to less effective classroom management and lower-quality instruction (Madigan & Kim, 2021). For students, distress can impede cognitive functions critical for language learning, such as memory, attention, and executive function, reducing their ability to absorb and use the new language (Tyng et al., 2017). This interdependence of well-being and educational outcomes necessitates a holistic approach that attends to the wellness of both educators and learners, ensuring that classrooms are not only places for linguistic development but also "spaces that promote a sense of safety and belonging, as well as meaningful, caring, respectful relationships among students and students-teachers" (Pentón Herrera, 2024, p. 205).

In this chapter, we broaden our conversation to encompass the concept of collective well-being, exploring its vital connection with SEL and holistic wellness. We will delve into the symbiotic relationship between individual wellness and the communal fabric of the classroom, underscoring how SEL can foster an environment where empathy, understanding, and cooperation are as integral to education as academic achievement. We examine the collaborative and communal aspects that are essential to both individual and collective success in language education, arguing that the path to linguistic proficiency is inextricably linked with nurturing the social and emotional fibers that bind us together as a learning community. By weaving SEL into the educational narrative, we aim to cultivate classrooms where collective well-being is elevated, creating a harmonious environment that bolsters both personal growth and academic excellence.

SEL SPOTLIGHT: ADAPTABILITY

Adaptability is an essential SEL skill in navigating the ups and downs of language acquisition. To promote adaptability, consider an activity that encourages students to embrace and learn from challenges. This SEL activity invites students to reflect on their adaptability through the lens of language learning:

- A challenge in my language learning journey that surprised me was (**situation**) _____
  _____
  _____

- My initial thoughts and feelings about this challenge were (**thoughts/emotions**) _____
  _____
  _____

- The steps I took to adjust and adapt included (**actions/skills**) ___
  _____
  _____
  _____

- Now I view changes in my learning process as (**perspective/ outcome**) _____
_____
_____

Invite students to share their reflections in pairs or groups, emphasizing the process of adapting to new challenges in language learning. This exercise allows students to articulate their personal growth stories and recognize the dynamic nature of learning a language. It also opens a dialogue about how adaptability is a key part of learning, enhancing their emotional intelligence and problem-solving skills. By integrating adaptability and other SEL skills in our practice, students improve their language abilities and cultivate a mindset that values flexibility and learning from experiences, thereby reinforcing the importance of overcoming challenges in both personal and academic realms.

Well-Being

The word *well-being* has become a buzzword in recent times, but what does it really mean? "Although well-being remains a difficult concept to define, specifically because of its intricate, multilayered nature, most readers will agree that it is essential for our happiness, flourishing, and successful development as human beings" (Pentón Herrera et al., 2023b, p. 2). There are many definitions and perspectives of well-being in contemporary conversations; however, for the purpose of our book, we use Pentón Herrera et al.'s definition. Well-being is:

> a state of equilibrium where individuals experience health, happiness, and prosperity, all of which lead to developing life satisfaction, self-realization, and the ability to engage in socially responsible behaviors—personally, professionally, emotionally, and spiritually— that produce long-lasting positive effects. Further, we hold that well-being is not an individual duty, but the responsibility of society and ecological systems where individuals reside as a whole. (2023b, p. 2)

At its core, well-being, sometimes used interchangeably with *wellness*, encompasses the emotional, psychological, and social conditions that contribute to individuals' overall satisfaction and happiness. From this perspective, emotional well-being pertains to how individuals perceive and react to their emotions, emphasizing the importance of self-regulation, awareness, and resilience in facing life's challenges (Ryff & Keyes, 1995). Psychological well-being extends beyond mere happiness to include aspects of personal growth, self-acceptance, autonomy, life purpose, environmental mastery, and the richness of one's relationships (Ryff, 1989). Lastly, social well-being reflects on our relationships and our role within the community, highlighting the value of social coherence and connectedness as integral components of a healthy, fulfilling life (Keyes, 1998). These three elements underscore the active pursuit of personal development and fulfillment as central to one's mental health. Nevertheless, emotional, psychological, and social conditions are not the only ones affecting an individual's well-being.

The conceptualization of well-being might be perceived or understood very differently depending on to whom we are talking. For example, according to Yale's School of Medicine, there are eight important dimensions of well-being that contribute to our wellness, as shown in Figure 6. Individuals hoping to achieve well-being should, then, consider which dimensions or elements are relevant in their lives and seek to find balance in those important areas.

An important note about well-being is that it should not be used interchangeably with the term *self-care*. When discussing the topic of well-being in the context of education, most scholars and educators have moved away from the term *self-care* as a way to critique the "sterile and impersonal practices" adopted by many school systems around the world, which places "the responsibility of being well on teachers alone" (Pentón Herrera et al., 2023b, p. 3). Self-care practices adopted in schools and education during the COVID-19 era (see Pentón Herrera et al., 2023b) often neglect the impact of systemic and environmental factors on personal health, inadvertently weaponizing self-care by placing undue emphasis on personal accountability at the expense of recognizing institutional responsibilities (Martínez-Alba et al., 2023). In recognition of these critiques, our approach in this book seeks to extend beyond the concept of individual self-care to examine how social structures, educational systems, and support networks contribute to and are accountable for the well-being of both educators and learners. This perspective encourages a more holistic view of well-being, one that integrates systemic and ecological solutions to complement personal strategies for managing and alleviating stress, preventing burnout, and promoting mental health.

While we are not psychologists or mental health experts, we strongly encourage educators to check in with themselves on a regular basis, perhaps using the wellness wheel below, and identify how they are feeling. Teaching is

Intellectual Wellness
The ability to open our minds to new ideas and experiences that can be applied to personal decisions, group interaction and community betterment.

Financial Wellness
The ability to identify your relationship with money and skills in managing resources. An intricate balance of the mental, spiritual, and physical aspects of money.

Emotional Wellness
The ability to understand ourselves and cope with the challenges life can bring.

Spiritual Wellness
The ability to establish peace and harmony in our lives.

Occupational Wellness
The ability to get personal fulfillment from our jobs or chosen career fields while still maintaining balance in our lives.

Physical Wellness
The ability to maintain a healthy quality of life without undue fatigue or physical stress.

Environmental Wellness
The ability to recognize our own responsibility for the quality of the environment that surrounds us.

Social Wellness
The ability to relate to and connect with other people in our world.

Figure 6: Wellness Wheel

hard, and life can sometimes bring unexpected challenges and obstacles that negatively impact our personal well-being. It is OK not to be OK all of the time. When we are struggling, the most important thing we can do is acknowledge those feelings. We can then reach out to available supports and resources in order to help attend to our personal needs. In all cases, we implore teachers not to be afraid to seek professional help if needed.

Well-Being in ELT

In the nascent literature on well-being within the domain of language education, early works predominantly tackled the subject ideologically (e.g., Hall & Eggington, 2000), focusing on the emotional challenges faced by non-native educators during instruction (Horwitz, 1996). At that time, the focus was mostly on students' unhelpful emotions, with little consideration given to understanding how these emotions were connected to students' overall well-being. Moreover, there was a notable lack of discussion regarding the well-being of teachers. Horwitz (1996) highlighted this oversight in the scholarly discourse, urging a more inclusive consideration of well-being that encompasses educators, noting the parallel harmful effects that undesired emotions, such as anxiety, could have on teachers and their instructional efficacy. In a related vein, one of the first studies to explicitly link well-being with academic performance in the context of ELT was Kao's (1999) research on the psychological well-being and educational achievement among immigrant youth. Kao discovered that despite the multitude of adversities immigrant youth navigate, a positive relationship exists between their psychological well-being and their academic success, underlining the significance of well-being as a determinant of educational outcomes.

In recent times, the discourse on well-being within the field of ELT has experienced substantial growth, with a broader recognition of the multifaceted influences on educators' well-being (Feryok, 2024; Mercer & Gregersen, 2020; Pentón Herrera et al., 2023a). Ardi et al. (2023) assert that both personal and systemic factors play significant roles in shaping teachers' mental health and job satisfaction. Contemporary research has moved beyond merely acknowledging the existence of stressors to actively exploring the interplay between educators' personal lives, institutional policies, and classroom practices. These advancements underline the importance of a supportive work environment, professional development opportunities, and recognition of teachers' efforts as integral to fostering their well-being. However, while teacher well-being has received increasing attention, the well-being of students in ELT contexts has remained comparatively underexplored. It is crucial to note that students' well-being is just as complex and significant as that of their instructors, and it warrants equal consideration. Language learners' emotional and psychological health can greatly impact their engagement, motivation, and, ultimately, their language acquisition (Mercer & Dörnyei, 2020). Therefore, future research and practice should aim to balance the focus, ensuring that the well-being of both students and teachers is nurtured, as their interdependent relationship is central to the success of the educational experience.

This growing body of work signifies a paradigm shift in ELT, advocating for comprehensive well-being strategies that address the needs of all stakeholders in the educational process (e.g., Yazan et al., 2023). One of the main takeaways from the current literature is the call for a systemic approach to well-being, one that integrates personal well-being management with structural and policy-level changes and responsibilities. This approach is about alleviating stress and cultivating an environment where teachers and students alike can thrive, thereby enhancing the overall quality of language education.

Well-Being in SEL

So, how does well-being connect to SEL? Well-being is a cornerstone concept in SEL, where it is recognized not just as an outcome but as a vital component of the educational process (Devaney & Moroney, 2018; Elias et al., 1997). SEL is predicated on the understanding that learning is intrinsically a social-emotional process, and as such, well-being must be nurtured to optimize educational outcomes. Research contends that SEL supports and benefits students' and teachers' well-being and growth (Ashdown & Bernard, 2012; Beard et al., 2023). This dual focus on skill development and well-being enrichment acknowledges the human aspect of education—the inherent social-emotional needs of those involved in teaching and learning. The significance of well-being within SEL is further illuminated by research indicating that emotional health is a predictor of academic performance (Pritchard & Wilson, 2003). When students feel well—when they are free from excessive stress, understand and manage their emotions, and experience beneficial relationships—they are more likely to engage deeply with learning materials and persist through challenges.

Moreover, the role of well-being in SEL extends beyond the classroom walls, affecting the broader school culture and the larger community.

A welcoming school climate, one in which every member's well-being is prioritized, fosters a sense of safety, belonging, and mutual respect. These conditions are essential for effective SEL, as they provide the stability and support necessary for students to take risks, engage in meaningful collaboration, and develop the skills needed for life beyond school (Cohen et al., 2009). Therefore, well-being in SEL is perceived as a holistic approach to cultivating capable and well-rounded individuals equipped to lead fulfilling lives. At the same time, while the promotion of well-being within SEL is foundational, it must be accompanied by a more nuanced understanding of its role and implications. It is not enough to endorse well-being as a standalone goal; the discourse must extend to how well-being integrates with and supports the objectives of SEL within the educational landscape and in the broader community context. We must probe the dynamics of well-being in SEL with critical questions, such as: Whose well-being is being served, and to what end? Who is included in our vision of well-being? Who decides what constitutes well-being? Ultimately, these and other critical questions could lead us to reflect on whether well-being is solely an individual pursuit or a collective responsibility that we share.

To expand on this perspective of well-being as both a personal responsibility and a collective duty, we employ Chambers's conceptualization of *responsible well-being* as a springboard. According to, Chambers, responsible well-being

> . . . recognizes obligations to others, both those alive and future generations, and to their quality of life. In general, the word "responsible" has moral force in proportion to wealth and power: the wealthier and more powerful people are, the greater the actual or potential impact of their actions or inactions, and so the greater the scope and need for their well-being to be responsible. Responsible well-being refers thus to doing as well as being; it is "by" as well as "for." The objective of development then becomes *responsible well-being by all and for all.* (1997, p. 1749)

According to Chambers, there are four elements that are essential to responsible well-being at the personal, societal, and global levels, including the environment:

- **Livelihood security:** *Livelihood* refers to having adequate resources to meet basic needs and to support well-being. *Security* refers to having the rights, safety, and access to live life with dignity. A sustainable livelihood is one that not only meets current needs without compromising the future but also continues to be productive over time. An equitable livelihood goes even further by contributing positively to the well-being of the wider community, ensuring that others can also achieve a good standard of living.

- **Capabilities:** "Capabilities refers to what people are capable of doing and being. They are means to livelihood and fulfillment; and their enlargement through learning, practice, training and education are means to better living and to well-being" (1997, p. 1748).
- **Equity:** *Equity* refers to the fair distribution of resources, opportunities, and care necessary for all individuals to achieve their full potential and well-being, without being disadvantaged by social, economic, or environmental factors. It emphasizes the ethical obligation to address disparities and ensure that every person has access to what they need for a healthy and fulfilling life.
- **Sustainability:** "Sustainability means that long-term perspectives should apply to all policies and actions, with sustainable well-being and sustainable livelihoods as objectives for present and future generations" (1997, pp. 1748–1749).

In our view, responsible well-being is the way forward in ELT and sister fields to achieve collective improvement in the quality of life and success of students, teachers, and stakeholders at large. Building on this point, we would like to clearly point out that the discourse on well-being within SEL often overlooks and fails to give voice to a critical group: teachers. When we advocate for teacher well-being through the prism of responsible well-being, we gain valuable insights into the widespread issue of teacher attrition. This perspective reveals how conventional educational models disproportionately burden teachers with the well-being of the school community—and everyone else (see Figure 7)—leading to undue stress and burnout. Such systemic pressures contribute significantly to teachers leaving the profession. Addressing this imbalance is essential for sustaining the well-being of educators and, by extension, the well-being of the entire educational ecosystem.

Through the lenses of SEL and responsible well-being, we can more clearly understand that this traditional approach to well-being does not work and is resulting in many of the challenges we continue to see in the field,

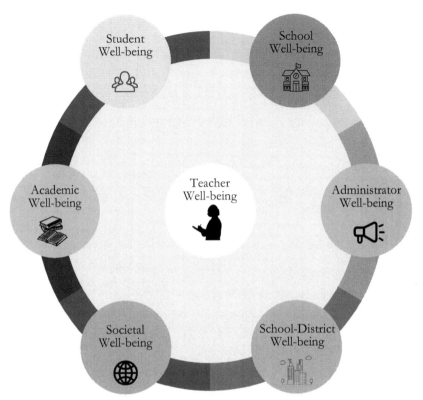

Figure 7: Traditional Conceptualization of Well-Being

Note: In this visual, we are depicting that in traditional school and social models, teachers are at the center of and are responsible for the well-being of the entire ecosystem and its stakeholders.

such as persistent high teacher attrition and low retention. In this traditional model of well-being:

- **Livelihood security:** Livelihood security is prioritized for students, to a certain extent, when it is concerned with the well-being of students when they are in the school building and are performing academically. However, teachers' rights, safety, and access to life with dignity remain on the decline and are widely invisible in conversations. As a matter of fact, teachers' rights (Strauss, 2023), safety (Peetz, 2023), and access (Berger, 2023) continue to decline. These factors greatly hinder teachers' ability to live life with dignity.

- **Capabilities**: Teachers are among the most prepared and well-educated members of society. Indeed, every profession in society owes its existence to the foundational work of teachers. This signifies that teachers are highly capable individuals who are expected to continuously engage in lifelong learning, practice, training, and education for the benefit of students and society as a whole. However, in many societies, the critical nature of teachers' roles is not fully recognized or valued as it should be. This undervaluation is evident in the persistently subpar worth (i.e., salary), prestige (i.e., respect), and value (i.e., investment) attributed to teachers and the teaching profession in many contexts today. Moreover, if teachers *do* seek professional development, they often have to pay for it themselves. In simple terms, teachers do not get paid based on the level of difficulty of the work they do but at the level of value society places on our profession.

- **Equity:** Equity in the educational sphere is critical, yet for many teachers it remains an unrealized ideal. Despite teachers' vital role in society, there is often a stark disparity in how resources and opportunities are allocated within the educational system. Teachers face inequities in pay, resources for professional development, and support compared to other professions requiring similar education and expertise levels. Such disparities undermine the teaching profession and reflect broader societal undervaluation of the contributions that teachers make to the future of communities and nations. Moreover, when teachers are not provided with the necessary conditions to achieve their full potential, it is not only their well-being that suffers but also the quality of education they can provide.

- **Sustainability:** When examining the long-term well-being of teachers at different educational levels, such as K-12, adult education, and higher education, it's apparent that the sustainability of teachers' careers has been largely overlooked. Current systemic practices often lead to educator burnout and attrition, challenging the notion of a sustainable teaching profession. Sustainable policies would necessitate not just the avoidance of burnout but also the creation of an environment where educators can grow and thrive over the course of their careers. This includes providing opportunities for professional advancement, ensuring a balanced workload, and creating a culture of appreciation that acknowledges teachers' integral role. Furthermore, sustainability in teaching must incorporate measures that encourage retention by addressing the financial, emotional, and professional needs of educators, thereby ensuring that their contributions to society can continue unabated for the benefit of future generations.

We believe, then, that responsible well-being in ELT—and education at large—would be better if teacher well-being is considered a collective responsibility of society. In Figure 8, we offer a visual representation of this perspective.

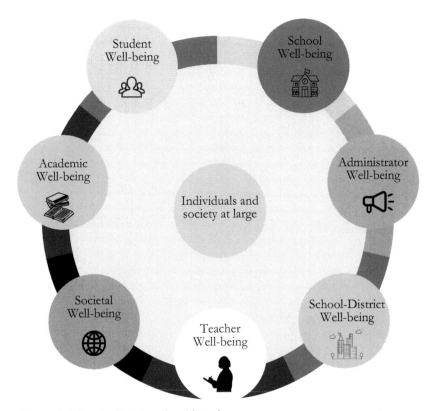

Figure 8: How Well-Being Should Look

Note: In this visual, we show how, through responsible well-being, the well-being of educational stakeholders, including teachers, is both a personal and collective responsibility.

Through the lens of responsible well-being, where personal and collective responsibility intertwine to create a harmonious educational ecosystem, these four pillars of well-being—livelihood security, capabilities, equity, and sustainability—could be re-envisioned as follows:

- **Livelihood security:** Livelihood security for educators is about creating a stable foundation where they can thrive alongside their students. In a well-balanced educational environment, teachers' rights and safety are not just protected; they are a priority. The discourse on ensuring a dignified professional life for educators is gaining momentum, signaling a move toward recognizing their pivotal role not only within schools but also in society. As we foster this security, we affirm that the well-being of teachers is as crucial as the academic performance of students, and we collectively commit to safeguarding it.

- **Capabilities**: Teachers are reservoirs of knowledge and skill, shaping the minds that will forge our future. As such, our continuous professional development is paramount. By investing in teachers' growth, we not only value their capabilities but also enhance the educational experiences of their students. Professional development should be encouraged and should not cause a financial burden on teachers. Societal appreciation of teachers' expertise should reflect a commitment to educational excellence. When teachers are supported to expand their skills and knowledge, the entire community stands to benefit from the ripple effect of empowered teaching.

- **Equity:** Equity in education for teachers means ensuring fair access to the resources and opportunities that allow us to perform at our best. It is a commitment to leveling the playing field and recognizing the invaluable service teachers provide. By aligning resources and support with teachers' needs, we acknowledge teachers' essential role in shaping a progressive society. Equity for educators leads to a more vibrant, effective educational system where all can thrive.

- **Sustainability:** The sustainability of the teaching profession is about nurturing an environment where educators' careers are not just endurable but fulfilling. Sustainable teaching practices ensure that educators have the space to innovate, connect, and inspire, day after day, year after year. By committing to the long-term well-being of teachers through supportive policies and a culture of respect, we lay the groundwork for a vibrant educational future. Moreover, affordable access to teacher preparation will encourage future educators to join the profession. This commitment is a testament to the value placed on those who educate, inspiring them to continue their vital work with passion and resilience.

SEL SPOTLIGHT: GOAL-SETTING

Goal-setting involves envisioning a desired outcome, planning ways to achieve it, and staying motivated throughout the process. In the context of language education, setting goals is not just about academic achievement; it is also a critical component of student well-being. By setting and pursuing goals, students can experience a sense of purpose and accomplishment that contributes to their overall happiness and satisfaction in learning.

The activity we share here seeks to encourage students to set personal well-being goals related to their language acquisition, helping them to connect their educational endeavors with their overall happiness and well-being.

- **Vision of Well-Being:** Begin by asking students to envision what well-being means to them in the context of language learning. **Prompt:** *When I think about being happy and fulfilled while learning a new language, I imagine myself _____ _____.*

- **Setting Specific Goals:** Guide students to set specific and achievable well-being goals for their language learning journey. **Prompt:** *A well-being goal I have for this language course/class is _____. This goal is important to me because _____ _____.*

- **Identifying Steps:** Have students identify concrete steps they can take to achieve their well-being goals. **Prompt:** *To reach my well-being goal, I will take the following steps: _____. I believe these actions will help me because _____ _____.*

- **Reflecting on Progress:** Encourage students to reflect on their progress toward their goals and to recognize any adjustments needed. **Prompt:** *As I work toward my goal, I have noticed _____. To continue making progress, I might need to _____.*

It is important for teachers to participate in this activity alongside their students, as a reflective practice and to model that these are important topics to reflect upon and revisit throughout our lives. Invite students to share their goals and plans with a partner or in small groups, fostering a supportive classroom environment where they can encourage and learn from one another. The teacher should join in with the sharing as well. Engaging in this practice of goal-setting not only sharpens linguistic competencies but also nurtures a resilient and growth-oriented mindset—a mindset that is important for both students and teachers to be better prepared for success. By intertwining goal-setting with other SEL skills, learners enhance their capacity to approach language acquisition with a balanced and reflective perspective. This holistic development is instrumental in affirming the symbiotic relationship between overcoming personal and academic hurdles and thriving within the multifaceted realm of language education.

Why Responsible Well-Being in ELT?

Although the ELT field is not new and has been alive and well for decades, we continue to struggle with the same issues of equity, support, access, and social justice. This is, perhaps, one of the reasons why we have become more active in ideological debates, arriving at the conclusions that all education is political and that teaching is a political act (Pennycook, 1989). In our fight toward a more equitable and just field, we have engaged in discussions and promoted new concepts and practices, such as translanguaging, the flipped classroom, positive psychology, teacher reflection, and many, many more. And yet, we continue to hear similar stories from teachers and students about injustices and lack of equity, support, and access. In our view, we need to rethink our approach to enhancing and helping the field move forward. We propose that responsible well-being should be the first and foundational step in every conversation surrounding ELT and sister fields because there is no success, innovation, or advancement without well-being.

The current global climate, marred by increased violence, turmoil, and instability, necessitates a model that not only addresses the intellectual development of students and educators but also their emotional and social health. The integration of SEL within ELT is not merely an additive component; it is a transformative approach that aligns with a holistic view of education, one that acknowledges the complex interplay between academic success and social and emotional welfare. Similarly, responsible well-being—a vital SEL pillar—in ELT calls for a reexamination of educational policies and practices, ensuring that they serve the dual purpose of fostering academic proficiency and nurturing well-being. In a time when educators and students face unprecedented challenges, the traditional metrics of educational success are no longer sufficient. The escalation of stressors within and outside school environments has been linked to a decline in mental health, underscoring the urgency for a shift that embeds well-being into the fabric of education.

In advocating for responsible well-being, we must confront the reality that education systems often reflect and perpetuate societal inequalities, including the systemic barriers that hinder the fulfillment and growth of students and educators. Advocacy for SEL and responsible well-being, therefore, becomes an advocacy for a more just and equitable society in which education plays a pivotal role in leveling the playing field. The call for responsible well-being in ELT is a call for humanity in education. While this charge may feel daunting, educators need not feel burdened to change entire systems in one day. Small acts can yield large results. While we might not be able to control our community, school district, or administrators, we can control our own interactions and the support we provide to our students and our colleagues. Also, we can share our knowledge regarding the importance of responsible well-being in our own contexts.

Motivated by the need to help the field move forward, and using Chambers's (1997) discussion on responsible well-being as a starting point, we propose the following model of responsible well-being, represented in Figure 9 and explained in Appendix 4. Our vision is that this model will be used by teachers, scholars, researchers, leaders, and any other stakeholders at any level of the ecosystem to evaluate how well-being is co-constructed responsibly in their educational environments.

SEL SPOTLIGHT: WELLNESS

Wellness is a multifaceted concept, encompassing physical, emotional, and mental health. In language learning, having the vocabulary to express various states of wellness can greatly enhance a student's ability to communicate their needs and experiences. This activity will help students identify and use new vocabulary related to wellness.

Wellness Word Map:

- **Step 1. Identifying Emotions and States:** Ask students to brainstorm words that relate to different aspects of wellness, such as *stress, balance, fatigue, joy,* or *satisfaction* in the context of their language learning journey. Encourage them to think about words that describe not only emotions but also physical sensations and mental states.
- **Step 2. Vocabulary Collection:** Students will then research and collect words and phrases that correspond to their brainstormed list. This can include synonyms, idioms, or expressions that native speakers might use to describe wellness.
- **Step 3. Mapping Wellness:** Each student will create a visual "Wellness Word Map." They can draw or use a digital graphic organizer to map out their collected vocabulary, categorizing the words by the aspect of wellness they represent (emotional, physical, mental).
- **Step 4. Personal Connection:** Have students choose words from their map that resonate with their personal experiences in language learning. They should prepare a short narrative or journal entry using these words to describe a time when their wellness was particularly strong or challenged.
- **Step 5. Group Reflection:** In pairs or small groups, students will share their Wellness Word Maps and narratives. This will give them the opportunity to discuss how they have used or could use the new vocabulary to communicate about wellness in their language learning and beyond.
- **Step 6. Class Vocabulary Bank:** As a class, compile a "Class Vocabulary Bank" of wellness terms. This resource will be a collective compilation that students can refer to when they need to articulate their state of wellness in the future.

This activity integrates vocabulary development with the exploration of wellness, providing students with the linguistic tools to express and discuss their well-being. It also fosters a supportive classroom environment where students learn from each other's insights and experiences related to wellness in language learning. We encourage teachers to engage in this activity alongside their students, contributing to the development of classroom community and modeling for students the importance of reflecting upon their own wellness throughout their lives.

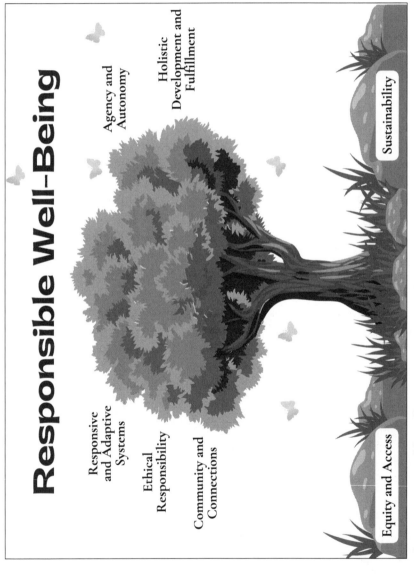

Figure 9: Responsible Well-Being

Final Thoughts

Reflecting on the transformative journey of responsible well-being, we return to Ms. Ali and Raúl fifteen years later. Ms. Ali is now the principal of the school. Her personal evolution mirrored the growth she fostered in her students, and now, as a leader, she has cultivated a school in which everybody has a fair opportunity (i.e., Equity and Access) to grow and succeed (i.e., Sustainability).

Raúl, once a student in Ms. Ali's classroom, has returned to these familiar halls as its youngest teacher. He carries with him the lessons about the need to build respectful relationships with students and colleagues (i.e., Community and Connections), which he learned under Ms. Ali's tutelage. His bright eyes, which once held stories of silent struggles, now sparkle with the enthusiasm of someone who has found his calling in the very environment that once nurtured his growth.

On a particularly sunny morning, Ms. Ali convenes the monthly faculty meeting. The room is filled with educators at various stages of their careers, each bringing unique perspectives and experiences to the gathering. In a gentle departure from the rigid structures of traditional meetings, Ms. Ali leads with a moment of breathing and reflection, a practice that has become a cornerstone of the school's culture (i.e., Holistic Development and Fulfillment).

As teachers open their eyes, Ms. Ali invites them to share their successes, small or large, personal or professional. The floor opens, and the room buzzes with stories of student breakthroughs and milestones. Raúl, with the humble confidence of a dedicated educator, shares an account of a student who, much like himself years ago, has overcome personal adversities to excel academically and socially. The success is not solely his but a testament to the nurturing environment that Ms. Ali has fostered, showcasing the importance of teachers' actions and practices (i.e., Agency and Autonomy) in the educational process.

Under Ms. Ali's leadership, the school has become a beacon of responsible well-being. Equity and access are not mere concepts but lived experiences, and sustainability initiatives are a visible and integral part of the school's operation and curriculum. These practices reflect the school's commitment to educating students in a manner that is fair, inclusive, and considerate of the broader community (i.e., Ethical Responsibility).

The pillars—Equity and Access, Sustainability—and tenets—Holistic Development, Community and Connections, Agency and Autonomy, and

Ethical Responsibility—of responsible well-being are the lived reality of the school, woven into the fabric of daily life. As the meeting concludes, the faculty leaves feeling acknowledged and supported, ready to continue their vital work, inspired by the knowledge that their well-being is as important to Ms. Ali as the educational mission they all share.

In this school, responsible well-being is the heartbeat, ensuring that every member, from the principal to the newest teacher, thrives. It is a place where education is more than knowledge transfer; it is about shaping well-rounded, responsible individuals ready to lead in a complex world.

Chapter 5
Future Directions for Social-Emotional Learning in Language Teaching

Introduction

Mr. Kovac, a veteran English teacher, is known in his high school community for his adherence to traditional teaching methods and a focus on academic rigor. Recently, the school implemented a district-wide SEL initiative to enhance students' social-emotional competencies. However, some teaching staff, including Mr. Kovac, met this initiative with apprehension and skepticism, believing that it would divert attention from academic content.

One of Mr. Kovac's students, Leila, is a bright but reserved student facing socioeconomic challenges that are affecting her school performance. Despite her interest in learning English, she struggles to engage fully due to the stresses in her life, which go unnoticed in the academically charged atmosphere of Mr. Kovac's classroom. One day, Mr. Kovac assigns a complex writing project, emphasizing the importance of factual accuracy and depth of research. Though intellectually stimulating, the assignment fails to consider students' varying personal backgrounds and emotional capacities.

As the deadline approaches, Leila finds herself overwhelmed. Her situation comes to light when Mr. Kovac notices her lack of participation, which is uncharacteristic. Prompted by a teacher-colleague who advocates for SEL, Mr. Kovac decides to have a one-on-one conversation with Leila. During their talk, Leila opens up about her struggles, explaining how external stressors have made it difficult for her to focus on her academic work. This revelation is a turning point for Mr. Kovac. He begins to see the value in understanding how students' backgrounds affect their social-emotional well-being and learning.

In response, Mr. Kovac adapts his teaching approach. He starts incorporating elements of SEL into his lessons, creating a more inclusive, supportive, and flexible classroom environment. This shift helps not only Leila but also the entire class. Students become more engaged, and the quality of their work improves, demonstrating that academic excellence and emotional well-being are not mutually exclusive but complementary.

SEL has become a focal point in modern discourse, though not without controversy. Its core tenet, the well-being of the educational community, has often been politicized, with detractors using it as a battleground to oppose broader social policies aimed at improving living conditions (Anderson, 2022). The contention around SEL reveals a deeper societal rift over the value placed on emotional and social well-being in education, often reflecting broader societal debates about equity and support for populations made vulnerable by the system. Critics may argue that SEL distracts from the "real" objectives of education, focusing on traditional academic outcomes that favor the banking model (Freire, 2000). However, this argument fails to acknowledge the substantial body of evidence illustrating that students' and teachers' well-being is inextricably linked to academic performance and professional efficacy (Mercer, 2021; Moreira-Sarmiento et al., 2022; Pentón Herrera, 2024). SEL is not a diversion from academic goals; rather, it is a foundational element that enables them. Well-being fosters an environment where learning can flourish, and individuals can achieve their full potential in the classroom and in life.

As we embark on Chapter 5—the concluding chapter of our exploration into the dynamic realm of SEL in ELT— it is essential to reflect on the transformative journey that has led us to the precipice of new horizons. From our initial foray into the foundational concepts of SEL, where we unpacked the essential elements and principles that underpin this vital aspect of education, to our deep dive into the critical role that SEL plays in the language classroom, each chapter has built upon the last to form a comprehensive understanding of the subject.

In Chapter 1, we explored the bedrock of SEL, understanding its intricate layers and how they converge to impact the learning experience. Chapter 2 expanded this understanding, situating SEL within the context of language teaching specifically and illuminating its significance in facilitating not just linguistic competence but also intercultural understanding and empathy. With Chapter 3, we moved from theory to practice, examining a range of strategies and activities designed to seamlessly weave SEL into the fabric of ELT, thereby enhancing both the teaching and learning experiences. Chapters 1 to 3 set the stage for Chapter 4, where we recognized the profound influence of SEL on collective well-being. We acknowledged that the social and emotional health of both educators and learners is not just an individual concern but a collective responsibility that bears on the entire educational ecosystem. Furthermore, we introduced and proposed responsible well-being as the way to move forward in our field. The realizations and lessons learned acquired throughout the chapters have, in our view, profound implications for the future of language education, calling for innovative approaches that prioritize the well-being of all stakeholders in the language learning process.

Now, as we approach the final chapter, we stand at the threshold of new beginnings. This chapter will not only consolidate the insights gleaned from our discussions but also chart a course for the pioneering work that lies ahead. We will address the potential challenges that may arise, consider the opportunities that await us in this evolving field, and explore the emerging paradigms that promise to reshape the landscape of SEL in ELT (and language teaching at large). Our goal is to extend an invitation to you, our readers, to join in a collaborative effort to propel the conversation forward. Together, we will envisage the future for SEL in language teaching—a future that embraces change, values emotional and social well-being, and recognizes the transformative power of education. This is more than a reflection on what has been; it is a call to action for what must be—a collective journey toward a future where language education is a conduit for nurturing compassionate global citizens equipped to thrive in an interconnected world.

As a final point, we would like to clarify and remind our readership that we are not mental health professionals. However, as ELT practitioners, we know and understand that mental health and well-being are at the forefront of our practice, and we feel it is our responsibility to be ready and prepared to support ourselves, our students, and our colleagues in need. In this book, we have written and approached the topic of SEL from our stance as English practitioners who infuse SEL and well-being into every part of our pedagogies and practices. We do so because, similar to Pentón Herrera and Martínez-Alba (2021), we believe that language classrooms are in a privileged position to incorporate SEL since language, emotions, and thoughts are very closely intertwined. At the same time, we acknowledge that there are limits to what "SEL can and should do for our students and teachers. SEL should never seek to replace professional mental health support or counseling services for students or teachers, and resources should be provided to those who need such support" (Pentón Herrera & Martínez-Alba, 2021, p. 107).

In the subsequent sections of this final chapter, we reflect on the challenges and possibilities moving forward. We know and understand that SEL is a very new field within ELT and language education at large. As such, we conclude by encouraging future discussions and mapping the evolving terrain of SEL in ELT.

Challenges

Research

One of the most pressing challenges that we face that is currently hindering the full integration of SEL within the sphere of ELT is the lack of current research in this field. As we stand in early 2024, the field has witnessed only a modest number of empirical studies explicitly exploring SEL in this context (e.g., Bai et al., 2021; Pentón Herrera, 2024; Soodmand Afshar et al., 2016; Suganda et al., 2018). And while it is important to highlight that there are empirical studies that could easily fit into the SEL category (e.g., Karam, 2021; Pentón Herrera, 2019; Pentón Herrera & Martínez-Alba, 2022), as they do not explicitly mention SEL, they may be harder for scholars interested in SEL to identify. And while it is promising that more books specific to SEL in teaching have been published in recent years, we argue that more empirical research is needed, like that found in the 2020 special issue of the *Journal of English Learner in Education* and the 2024 issue of *Anglica: An International Journal of English Studies*.

Research can help not only to inform teaching practices but also to add more evidence to validate the effectiveness of SEL for students in the ELT classroom. As we endeavor to bridge the research gap, it is critical to propose focused agendas that will invigorate scholarly inquiry into SEL within ELT. Future research could explore how SEL strategies impact language acquisition and retention in diverse educational settings. Studies might investigate the efficacy of SEL integration in language curriculum and its influence on students' linguistic confidence and intercultural competence. Additionally, longitudinal research could examine the long-term benefits of SEL on learners' personal and academic trajectories. Potential research questions to stimulate scholarly exploration include:

- How do specific SEL interventions influence the motivation and engagement of language learners from various cultural backgrounds?
- What are the effects of SEL on teacher-student and student-student interactions and classroom dynamics in ELT?
- In what ways can SEL practices be tailored to support students with different proficiency levels and learning needs?
- How do online and hybrid learning environments affect the implementation and outcomes of SEL in language education?

There is no doubt that SEL researchers face challenges. Not only is SEL a burgeoning field, but the term *social-emotional learning* has also been found to be contentious and used in political debates regarding policies and practices in K-12 schools across the United States specifically, with some parents and politicians spreading misunderstanding about SEL being a vehicle for indoctrinating students. This, coupled with the fact that often journal editors and/or peer reviewers do not know or fully comprehend what SEL is and what it is not, should only further fuel our efforts to conduct and publish research on this topic.

Practical Resources

Although some practical resources have been published in recent times (e.g., Martínez-Alba & Pentón Herrera, 2023; Mueller & Pentón Herrera, 2023; Pentón Herrera, 2020; Pentón Herrera & Martínez-Alba, 2021), as a field, we still face a significant shortfall in practical SEL resources that adequately cater to the diverse spectrum of age, culture, and language proficiency levels in our classrooms. This scarcity is particularly felt in teacher preparation programs, where the need to equip future language educators with the tools to implement SEL in their classrooms is critical. The breadth of language learners, ranging from young children to adults, and the rich tapestry of cultural backgrounds call for materials that are not only flexible and adaptive but also deeply informed by cultural competencies. Language proficiency levels, which vary widely, necessitate SEL resources that can support and enhance language learning at every stage, providing relevant and effective scaffolding that resonates with students' linguistic abilities and life experiences.

In response to this need, there is a pressing call for the development of comprehensive SEL materials for language educators and teacher educators alike. These resources should be wide-ranging, including curricula that integrate SEL into teacher training programs and continuous professional development for practicing teachers. For example, in language teacher preparation programs, specifically, textbooks could address the effect of well-being, identity, and emotions on teachers' performance and students' achievement, as in the example of Pentón Herrera and Martínez-Alba (2022). Similarly, professional development for pre- and in-service teachers could delve into the need to understand and develop emotional intelligence in language learning spaces, as suggested by Hasper (2023). Collaborative efforts to create these materials should involve diverse stakeholders to ensure that the resulting products are pedagogically robust, culturally attuned, and practical for real-world application. By weaving SEL into the fabric of teacher education and language teaching, we can empower educators and students at all levels to co-create supportive, empathetic, and responsive language learning environments, ultimately enriching the educational experience for both teachers and learners.

Moving Beyond "One-Size-Fits-All"

The notion of a "one-size-fits-all" approach to SEL within diverse educational landscapes is increasingly recognized as inadequate. Current SEL approaches, while foundational, often fall short of addressing the nuanced needs of varied learning environments and cultural contexts. These models can inadvertently overlook the specific social-emotional dynamics of different student populations, particularly when they are transplanted wholesale from one educational system to another without due consideration for cultural relevance and adaptability. For example, while poetry and storytelling might be effective in contexts that welcome personal expression and creativity, they may not meet the needs of students in highly structured and analytical academic contexts. The premise that a single SEL framework can be universally applicable underestimates the complex interplay of cultural norms, educational traditions, and linguistic nuances that influence how SEL should be integrated into language education. Such a critique urges us to reconsider and refine SEL approaches to ensure that they are genuinely inclusive and responsive to the rich diversity of global educational contexts.

In response to these limitations, it is essential to develop and offer alternatives that allow for adaptable and flexible SEL implementations in language teaching, keeping in mind that SEL is a pedagogical approach, not a program. These alternatives should emphasize a bottom-up approach that takes root in the specificities of each educational setting, harnessing insights from educators, learners, and communities to tailor SEL practices that align with local cultural values and educational goals. For instance, modular SEL curricula that educators can customize, incorporating a mix of global perspectives and local wisdom, could be one such alternative (see Mesinas & Casanova, 2023). The creation of collaborative platforms where teachers can share and co-create SEL materials and strategies that speak to their unique teaching situations is another. This co-creation process should be supported by robust professional development programs that equip teachers with the skills to critically assess and adapt SEL resources, ensuring that the social and emotional growth fostered in language classrooms worldwide is as diverse and dynamic as the students themselves.

Streamlining SEL Integration

A prevailing myth about SEL in language education is that it places an excessive burden on educators, adding to an already full workload. However, this misconception stems from a misunderstanding of SEL as an add-on rather than an integral component of effective teaching. The truth is that when SEL is woven into the fabric of classroom interactions and lesson plans, it enhances rather than encumbers the teaching process. Educators often practice aspects of SEL intuitively, such as fostering a supportive classroom environment or encouraging collaboration. The key is not to view SEL as a separate task but as a natural extension of good teaching practices that can actually streamline classroom management and improve student engagement, thereby reducing overall teacher workload.

To integrate SEL effectively without overwhelming existing responsibilities, educators can employ strategies that dovetail with their routine pedagogical tasks. As we described in Chapter 3, this can include aligning SEL objectives with language learning goals (see also Pentón Herrera and Martínez-Alba 2021), such as using group activities that promote teamwork while practicing conversational skills. Teachers can also incorporate SEL into assessment by reflecting on students' collaborative skills and emotional intelligence as part of project evaluations (see Chapter 3, and Appendices 2 and 3).

Professional development should focus on practical SEL applications that fit organically within existing lesson plans, highlighting that SEL is not about doing more but about teaching smarter. By reframing SEL implementation as a series of small manageable adjustments to teaching methods, educators can enrich their classrooms with minimal additional effort.

Possibilities

Holistic Affective Education

We encourage the ELT community to consider a holistic affective education curriculum; emotions are not merely feelings to be discussed but the compass that guides the learning process, signaling connections and enhancing memory. Similarly, agency becomes the driving force, enabling learners to make choices about their language learning journey and fostering independence and responsibility. Furthermore, the integration of well-being into this educational approach is crucial, as it ensures that learners' mental, emotional, and social health are nurtured, contributing to their overall resilience and satisfaction in the learning environment. This curriculum is not structured in silos but is interlaced with opportunities for students to reflect on their personal histories, cultural backgrounds, and aspirations, thus shaping their learning experience to be as unique as their fingerprints. Within this framework, language could become a tool not just for communication but for self-expression and personal growth, facilitating an exploration of self alongside the acquisition of linguistic skills.

The benefits of such an integrative approach to learners' development could be multifold. By acknowledging and nurturing the whole person, the curriculum could support not just cognitive but also social and emotional growth. Learners equipped with a strong sense of identity can navigate the intricacies of global communication with confidence and authenticity. The emotional intelligence fostered through this approach empowers them to connect with others meaningfully, transforming interactions into rich learning experiences. Moreover, by prioritizing well-being, this approach ensures that students are not only academically prepared but also emotionally resilient, capable of maintaining a healthy balance in their personal and professional lives. The cultivation of agency instills in learners a proactive stance toward their education, preparing them to become lifelong learners who can adapt to an ever-changing world. Holistic affective education thus could be the next step in language education toward preparing students for academic success and for a life of purposeful engagement in today's globalized society.

Cross-Cultural Competence and SEL

SEL serves as a powerful conduit for enhancing cross-cultural understanding, providing a framework that goes beyond the acquisition of linguistic competence to foster a deeper appreciation for diversity. Through SEL, learners are encouraged to engage with empathy, to listen actively, and to understand perspectives that differ from their own. This engagement is not limited to the cognitive understanding of cultural differences but extends to a heartfelt appreciation of the myriad ways in which people experience and interact with the world. SEL promotes the development of skills such as perspective-taking and emotional literacy, which are essential for navigating and appreciating the complex social tapestries of different cultures. By integrating SEL into the language curriculum, students learn to communicate effectively across cultural boundaries, developing fluency not just in language but also in the nuanced dance of intercultural relations.

The role of language teachers is pivotal in embedding cross-cultural competency in SEL. Educators are the architects of the learning environment, and by embedding principles of SEL into their teaching, they can design experiences that consciously build cross-cultural connections. Language teachers can create scenarios that challenge students to apply their social and emotional understanding within culturally diverse contexts, thereby strengthening their intercultural competency. Through activities that promote collaboration and reflection, teachers enable students to examine and bridge cultural divides, fostering a classroom culture that values and celebrates diversity. By championing SEL, language teachers empower their students to become culturally competent communicators who can thrive in a globally interconnected society.

SEL and Ecological Literacy in ELT

The integration of SEL with ecological literacy in ELT presents an innovative pathway for educators to nurture well-rounded learners who are attuned to the environmental challenges of our times. By incorporating SEL and ecological education in ELT, we equip students with the emotional tools to understand and empathize with the planet's plight, fostering a sense of stewardship that transcends the classroom. This synergistic approach enables learners to process complex ecological concepts through the lens of SEL, where the emotional resonance of environmental issues becomes a powerful motivator for learning and action. Students are thus prepared not only to articulate their thoughts on ecological matters but also to internalize and respond to them with emotional intelligence and a sense of responsibility. The resulting educational experience is one that cultivates a deep connection between the learner, the language, and the living world, empowering students to become advocates for sustainability and change within their communities and beyond.

Teaching practices that intertwine ecological themes with linguistic tasks can effectively cultivate SEL competencies such as collaboration and empathy. For example, one such practice could involve problem-based service-learning (PBSL; see Aker et al., 2018), in which students collaborate to solve real-world environmental problems, using the target language as their medium of communication. Also, educators could incorporate projects that range from local community initiatives to virtual exchanges with students from different parts of the world, focusing on global environmental challenges. Through these collaborative efforts, students practice and develop skills in empathy by considering diverse perspectives on ecological issues and in teamwork by uniting to find solutions. Similarly, storytelling or story-based learning, where students create and share stories related to environmental experiences, can lead to a deeper understanding and personal connection with ecological themes in general and the environmental needs of their own communities specifically. This narrative approach fosters empathy and self-reflection, allowing students to explore the emotional dimensions of ecological issues while developing their language proficiency.

Global Citizenship and SEL Integration

SEL is pivotal in cultivating global citizenship, as it lays the foundation for empathy, open-mindedness, and collaborative problem-solving—skills imperative for international cooperation and understanding. By integrating SEL into the curriculum, educators can foster a learning environment that encourages students to appreciate and navigate the complexities of a diverse world. This integration enables students to understand global issues not just intellectually but also emotionally, giving rise to a form of global awareness that encompasses a sense of justice, equity, and compassion. SEL's focus on emotional intelligence and empathy becomes a conduit through which learners can appreciate their roles as global citizens, equipping them with the necessary skills to engage in cross-cultural dialogue, conflict resolution, and cooperative efforts that address global challenges.

Language programs designed with a global perspective do more than teach communication; they serve as platforms for learners to understand their roles and responsibilities within an interconnected global community. Such programs should encourage learners to explore cultural narratives, engage in discussions about global issues, and participate in simulations that mirror real-world international collaborations. These experiences, framed within the context of language learning, allow students to practice linguistic skills while also developing an understanding of global cultures and perspectives. By emphasizing the shared responsibilities of environmental stewardship, social justice, and cultural exchange, language educators can help students develop a sense of interconnectedness, preparing them to act with agency and empathy in the global arena. The ultimate goal of SEL in ELT should be to shape individuals who are not only proficient in language but also committed to the collective well-being of the global community.

Digital and Media Integration

In the age of digital learning, the use of digital tools and media offers unprecedented opportunities to promote SEL within language education. Digital platforms can provide dynamic, interactive environments that encourage self-expression, empathy, and social interaction—core components of SEL. For example, online forums and social media groups can be utilized to foster discussions around language content that also touch upon cultural understanding and emotional intelligence. Language learning apps with gamification elements can motivate students through challenges that require teamwork and communication, reinforcing SEL principles. Additionally, digital storytelling tools enable learners to craft narratives that explore personal and social themes, providing a canvas for emotional expression and cultural exchange. These digital avenues not only enhance language skills but also cultivate the SEL competencies necessary for students to navigate the complex social landscapes of the digital world.

Effective integration of technology in SEL can be demonstrated through various practices. One such example is the use of virtual reality (VR) in language classes, where learners engage in immersive cultural experiences that evoke empathy and deepen their understanding of diverse perspectives. Another example might involve collaborative projects using digital platforms like Padlet or Google Classroom, where students from different parts of the world work together on environmental projects, discussing and negotiating in the target language, which fosters cross-cultural understanding and global awareness. Blogs and video diaries have also been used as reflective tools, allowing students to articulate their emotional journeys in learning a new language, thus connecting the cognitive aspects of language learning with emotional and social growth. With new technologies being created and available to teachers and learners every day, the possibilities are endless. These examples illustrate the power of technology to enhance SEL in language learning, creating rich, authentic contexts for students to develop not just language proficiency but also the emotional and social skills that are essential in today's interconnected world.

Student-Centered Pedagogical Models

Innovative pedagogical models that prioritize SEL are transforming the educational landscape, particularly within language teaching. Service learning, for example, integrates meaningful community service with instruction and reflection, fostering a heightened sense of social responsibility and personal growth. In the language classroom, this might involve students engaging in projects that benefit both the local and international community, using their language skills to advocate for social issues or to support speakers of other languages. Similarly, reflective practices such as journaling, peer feedback sessions, and guided meditations are being incorporated into curriculums to encourage mindfulness and self-awareness. These practices allow learners to connect their language learning with personal values and community engagement, thereby fostering a deeper, more empathetic understanding of both self and others within the learning process.

Implementing these SEL-centered pedagogical models in diverse teaching contexts requires careful consideration of cultural, institutional, and individual learner differences. Educators should start by creating a supportive environment that values and encourages open communication and reflection. This could be facilitated by regular class discussions that allow students to share their experiences and learn from each other. When it comes to service-learning, it is important to collaborate with community partners to ensure that the service provided meets real needs and offers genuine learning opportunities. For reflective practices, educators must provide clear guidelines and prompts to guide students' reflection, while also respecting students' privacy and personal boundaries. Flexibility is key; these models should be adaptable to various learning settings, whether in-person, online, or hybrid, and should be tailored to fit the unique cultural and linguistic backgrounds of the learners.

Maintaining Relevance

In a rapidly transforming educational environment, the necessity of evolving SEL practices cannot be overstated. As educators, there is a pressing need to continuously adapt SEL methodologies to align with technological advancements, changing social dynamics, and the shifting needs of learners. This evolution is essential not only for maintaining the relevance of SEL but also for enhancing its impact in fostering resilient, empathetic, and socially adept individuals. Educational paradigms now require SEL to be flexible enough to accommodate blended learning environments, culturally diverse classrooms, and the digital communication norms of the twenty-first century. By staying attuned to these changes and evolving accordingly, SEL can continue to play a crucial role in helping students navigate the complexities of modern life and education.

For educators to stay informed and ensure the ongoing relevance of SEL in their teaching practices, a proactive approach is needed. This includes engaging in continuous professional development, participating in SEL-focused workshops, and collaborating with a community of practice. Educators should also be encouraged to integrate current research findings into their SEL applications, tailoring practices to reflect contemporary societal issues and educational trends. Furthermore, adopting a reflective teaching practice is vital, where educators regularly assess the effectiveness of their SEL integration and make data-informed adjustments. Utilizing social media and professional networks to share insights and strategies can also provide a dynamic platform for educators to keep abreast of innovative SEL methodologies. Ultimately, the goal is to create a responsive SEL framework that supports the holistic development of learners and prepares them to thrive in an ever-changing world.

Final Thoughts

As we draw to the end of our journey exploring the multifaceted realm of SEL in the context of language teaching, we find ourselves at a vantage point that offers both a reflection of the past and a gateway to the future. In this book, we have shared our insights and experiences highlighting the profound integration of SEL within the sphere of language education.

Throughout these five chapters, we have intimately explored SEL—from its foundational principles to its pivotal role in shaping empathetic and interculturally competent language learners. Our firsthand experiences with SEL have shown us its power in fostering empathy, resilience, and bridging cultural gaps inside and outside learning spaces. Yet our quest for a more socially and emotionally conscious approach to language education remains steadfast.

We hope this book serves as a clarion call, urging you, our readers, to become a vanguard of this transformative movement. Our vision is that you will take the insights shared throughout our conversations, infuse them into your own contexts, and contribute to the burgeoning research and practices that will propel SEL forward. Your commitment and advocacy toward embracing SEL are pivotal in shaping the narrative of language education, ensuring that it evolves to meet the exigencies of our times.

As we part ways at the conclusion of this manuscript, let us anchor ourselves in an optimistic vision—the belief in the transformative power of SEL not only to craft proficient language users but also to nurture individuals who are empathetic, culturally attuned, and engaged in the global dialogue with heart and mindfulness. We exhort you to keep championing SEL in our classrooms and beyond. SEL is the most vital ingredient to turn language learning into a path for shaping kind, connected global citizens, all set to make their mark in our tight-knit world. Here's to that future—let's make it happen!

Appendix 1

Considerations for Teaching Emotional Skills

Teaching emotional skills, be it literacy or intelligence, requires a thoughtful approach that recognizes the diverse emotional needs and backgrounds of students. When integrating these teachings into classrooms, especially language classrooms, educators might consider the following:

- **Tailored Activities:** Customize emotional learning exercises based on the age group, cultural background, and individual needs of the students.
- **Safe Environments:** Create a classroom setting where students feel safe to express, share, and explore their emotions without judgment.
- **Incorporate Storytelling:** Use stories, narratives, or real-life scenarios that resonate with students, prompting them to identify and discuss the emotions embedded in these tales.
- **Interactive Games:** Design games that encourage students to recognize, name, and discuss different emotions. This can be particularly effective in language classrooms, intertwining emotional vocabulary with language learning.
- **Reflection Time:** Allocate time for students to reflect on their emotional experiences and responses. This introspection can be facilitated through journal writing, group discussions, or one-on-one conversations.
- **Modeling:** Act as a role model, displaying emotional literacy and intelligence in interactions. Show students the appropriate ways to react, empathize, and communicate emotions.

Appendix 2

Approaches to Teaching Emotional Skills in Language Classrooms

In language classrooms, mastering vocabulary, grammar, and syntax is just one part of effective communication. True proficiency comes when students can also understand and convey emotions in their newfound language, adapting to cultural nuances and contexts. By embedding emotional literacy and intelligence within language teaching methodologies, educators can offer students a more holistic language learning experience. The following teaching approaches have been selected as examples of how we can teach emotional skills to our students in language classrooms:

- **Emotion-Driven Role-Playing:** Incorporate role-playing activities in which students enact scenarios to express and interpret various emotions. This technique enhances both verbal and nonverbal emotional communication. See Cahnmann-Taylor and McGovern (2021) for examples and inspiration.
- **Emotion Vocabulary Lists:** Create thematic vocabulary lists or flashcards centered around different emotions. For instance, the theme "Happiness" could include words like *elated, joyful,* and *content.* See Brackett's (2019) book for a list of emotion vocabulary.
- **Reflective Journals:** Encourage students to maintain journals where they can document and reflect upon their daily emotional experiences. This cultivates self-awareness and fosters emotional literacy. See Mueller and Pentón Herrera (2023) for an example.
- **Discussion Circles:** Regularly engage students in group discussions about emotions they encounter in readings, movies, or real-life experiences. This promotes empathy and the ability to recognize emotions in others. See Pentón Herrera and McNair (2021) and McNair and Pentón Herrera (2022) for examples.
- **Emotion Recognition Games:** Organize activities where students guess the emotions being portrayed by their peers, helping them improve their intuitive understanding of emotional cues. See Giroux (2022) for more details.

- **Mindfulness Practices:** Integrate simple mindfulness exercises at the beginning or end of lessons. Techniques such as deep breathing or guided imagery can teach students to manage their emotions and remain centered. See Pentón Herrera and Martínez-Alba (2021) for examples and lessons.
- **Emotion-Based Storytelling:** Assign storytelling tasks where students create narratives centered around specific emotions, allowing them to delve deep into the nuances of emotional experiences. See Martínez-Alba and Pentón Herrera (2023) for examples.
- **Feedback Sessions:** Post-activity discussions in which students express how they felt during an exercise can be invaluable. It not only aids in emotional recognition but also emphasizes the importance of managing and expressing those feelings appropriately.
- **Scenario Analysis:** Present students with various hypothetical situations, asking them to predict emotional reactions or suggest emotionally intelligent responses.
- **Cultural Emotion Exploration:** Since emotional expressions can vary across cultures, engage students in exploring how different cultures express and interpret emotions. This can be particularly beneficial in a diverse language classroom. See Alber (2021) and Pentón Herrera (2019) for examples.

Appendix 3
Full Version of Lesson Plan

Topic: Building teamwork and respecting differences through literature

Language Objectives:

- Students will be able to collaboratively write a short story in small groups.
- Students will be able to present their story orally to the class.

Content Objectives:

- Students will be able to identify and discuss the importance of teamwork in different contexts.
- Students will be able to recognize and appreciate individual differences in their peers' contributions.

SEL Competencies:

- Students will be able to understand teamwork and work with others.
- Students will respect individual differences.
- These two competencies come from the Employability skills identified above.

Materials:

- Short stories (some possible options):
    - The bundle of sticks (a classic fable emphasizing unity)
    - *The Day the Crayons Quit* by Drew Daywalt (a story about different crayons expressing their individual perspectives)
    - *Swimmy* by Leo Lionni (a tale about a small fish's teamwork to overcome a bigger challenge)

- *Stone Soup* (a folktale about a community coming together, each contributing a small part)
- Collaborative writing worksheet: This will have sections for:
  - Title of the story
  - Setting
  - Main characters
  - Plot (beginning, middle, end)
  - Lesson/moral of the story
- Presentation tools: Whiteboard, markers, projector, microphone, laptop, etc.
- Reflection worksheet: Questions might include:
  - How did your group demonstrate teamwork while creating your story?
  - What differences did you notice in your group members, and how did these contribute to the story?
  - What was the most challenging part of this activity, and how did you overcome it?
  - How will you apply what you learned about teamwork and individual differences in real-life situations?

Procedure:

- Warm-up discussion:
  - Can you think of a time when teamwork helped you achieve something?
  - Why is it important to recognize and appreciate the different skills and perspectives of your teammates?
- Discussion after reading the class story:
  - How did the characters in the story demonstrate teamwork?
  - What were the individual differences you noticed among the characters, and how did these influence the story?
  - If you were in the story, how would you have contributed to the team?
- Group writing activity:
  - Remember to incorporate elements of teamwork and individual differences in your story.
  - Think about a challenge your characters might face and how they can overcome it together.

Assessments (rubrics provided on the next page):

- Story assessment rubric. Categories might include:
  - Incorporation of teamwork elements
  - Recognition of individual differences
  - Story structure and cohesiveness
  - Creativity and originality
- Presentation evaluation sheet. Categories can be:
  - Clarity of presentation
  - Collaboration among group members
  - Relevance to lesson objectives
  - Audience engagement
- Reflection prompts:

  - What did you learn from this activity about the importance of teamwork?
  - How can you apply the values of teamwork and respecting individual differences in your daily life?

Extensions:

- Creative expression: Invite students to create a visual representation (like a comic strip or poster) of their story, highlighting the elements of teamwork and individual differences.
- Drama extension: Encourage students to convert their written story into a short skit or play, emphasizing nonverbal communication and collaboration during the performance.
- Literary exploration: Ask students to find examples of teamwork and individual differences in books they have read or movies they have watched. They can write a brief report or give a short presentation on their findings.

Differentiation:

- For emerging readers/writers: Provide sentence starters or a story template for students to use when writing their collaborative story. Additionally, allow the use of storytelling cards or visuals to help them structure their story.

- For advanced learners: Challenge them to incorporate specific literary devices into their stories, such as foreshadowing, metaphor, or symbolism. They can also be tasked with identifying these devices in the initial class story read-aloud.
- For visual or kinesthetic learners: Offer the option of creating a storyboard, collage, or physical reenactment of their story, highlighting the themes of teamwork and individual differences.
- For auditory learners: Encourage these students to focus on the oral presentation aspect.

Story Assessment Rubric

Criteria	Excellent (5)	Good (4)	Satisfactory (3)	Needs Improvement (1–2)
Incorporation of teamwork elements	Demonstrates a clear and profound understanding of teamwork through the narrative	Includes good examples of teamwork but may lack depth; could be developed more	Shows signs of teamwork, but may be vague, superficial, or underdeveloped	Minimal or no clear representation of teamwork incorporated
Recognition of individual differences	Skillfully highlights diverse characters and their unique contributions	Recognizes differences but may not deeply explore them; could be developed more	Instances of individuality and differences are present but may be limited or underdeveloped	No clear representation of individual differences recognized
Story structure and cohesiveness	Strong beginning, middle, and end with seamless transitions	Generally well-structured but may have minor gaps; could be developed more	Adequate structure but may have gaps, lack smooth flow, or could be developed more	Progression is unclear or confusing; beginning, middle, end, and/or transitions may be underdeveloped, unclear, or missing

Criteria	Excellent (5)	Good (4)	Satisfactory (3)	Needs Improvement (1–2)
Creativity and originality	Unique and innovative story concept; engaging from start to finish; no borrowed concepts or clichés	Creative ideas included in the story, but may also have a few borrowed concepts or clichés	Story contains some original elements, but also relies on predictable elements, borrowed concepts, or clichés	Story lacks creativity. Ideas are largely predictable, are borrowed concepts or clichés

Presentation Evaluation Sheet

Criteria	Excellent (5)	Good (4)	Satisfactory (3)	Needs Improvement (1–2)
Clarity of presentation	Clear, articulate, and well-paced delivery	Delivery is mostly clear with occasional stumbles; pacing may be too fast or too slow, hindering understanding and enjoyment	Presentation includes parts that are clear and parts that are difficult to follow. Many stumbles occur or pacing may be too fast or too slow, making it significantly difficult to understand and enjoy	Presentation is difficult to follow; many clarity or pacing issues making the presentation almost impossible to understand

Criteria	Excellent (5)	Good (4)	Satisfactory (3)	Needs Improvement (1–2)
Collaboration among group members	Equal, positive, professional collaboration among group members is evident	Collaboration among group members is satisfactory, yielding a positive end result	Collaboration among group members may have some challenges that detract from the end result; some group members may not participate equally	Lack of collaboration; collaboration among group members negatively affects the end result; group members do not participate equally
Relevance to lesson objectives	Directly aligns with objectives; exceptionally relevant	Good alignment but may drift off topic occasionally	Somewhat relevant but may lack depth or have components that are not clearly aligned	Lesson is unrelated or not aligned with identified lesson objectives
Audience engagement	Engages audience throughout; strong rapport	Engages audience for most of the presentation	Attempts to engage audience are made but are largely unsuccessful; some parts may lack interest	Little to no audience engagement

Reflection Worksheet

Name: _____ Date: _____

Please answer the following questions thoughtfully:

What did you learn from this activity about the importance of teamwork?

_____

_____

_____

_____

_____

_____

How can you apply the values of teamwork and respecting individual differences in your daily life?

_____

_____

_____

_____

_____

_____

Appendix 4

Responsible Well-Being

Pillars

- **Equity and Access:** Equity and access refer to ensuring that both students and educators have fair opportunities and resources to engage in and facilitate learning. This involves creating an inclusive environment where the diverse needs and backgrounds of both students and teachers are acknowledged and accommodated. For students, this entails the provision of a quality education that includes access to robust learning materials, resources, and support systems that respect and address socioeconomic, cultural, or physical differences. Equity for students means that each learner is given what they need to succeed to the best of their abilities within the educational setting. For teachers, the principle of equity and access extends to valuing their profession and uplifting their role in society. This means recognizing that teachers are fundamental to societal development and well-being. It is imperative to provide them with continuous professional development opportunities, adequate compensation, and the resources necessary to meet the varying demands of their roles. Societal appreciation for teachers must be reflected in how their work is supported and facilitated, understanding that their well-being has a profound impact on their ability to foster a nurturing and effective learning environment. This pillar of responsible well-being underscores the symbiotic relationship between student learning and teacher welfare. It posits that equitable support for teachers is not just about providing tools for instruction but also about elevating the respect and recognition they receive, which in turn benefits the broader educational community. By prioritizing both the social, emotional, and professional needs of teachers alongside the academic and emotional needs of students, an educational ecosystem that is conducive to the growth and well-being of all its members can be cultivated.

- **Sustainability:** Sustainability refers to the creation and maintenance of systems that are environmentally sound, economically viable, and socially equitable, ensuring resilience and continuity over time. For students, sustainability means embedding environmental and social responsibility into the curriculum, equipping them with the knowledge and skills to navigate and shape a rapidly changing world. It involves preparing them to think critically about global issues, to act with consideration for ecological balance, and to engage as proactive stewards of a sustainable future. For teachers, sustainability extends to being given the resources needed to create a supportive professional ecosystem that values and nurtures their well-being and career longevity. This encompasses providing opportunities for learning and growth, ensuring job security, maintaining dignity and pride, and fostering work environments that promote mental and physical health. It also involves acknowledging the critical role that educators play in shaping future generations and ensuring that they are equipped with the resources and support needed to teach sustainability concepts effectively. Sustainability in education also signifies the interdependence of educational systems with the broader ecological, economic, and social systems. It advocates for operational practices within schools and educational institutions that minimize environmental impact, promote economic efficiency, and contribute positively to the community. This includes incorporating projects and learning that reinforce the real-world application of sustainability. This pillar of responsible well-being commits to a vision where the vitality and integrity of the educational process are preserved for present and future generations. It calls for an intentional and collaborative effort to craft an education system that not only endures but also evolves in harmony with our planet and society. By fostering a culture of sustainability, educators and learners become co-creators in a legacy that transcends the classroom, ensuring that the educational endeavor continues to be a source of personal fulfillment, professional satisfaction, and societal advancement.

Tenets

- **Holistic Development and Fulfillment:** This tenet emphasizes the comprehensive growth of individuals—both learners and educators. It advocates for the need for a broad-based development that includes cognitive, emotional, social, and physical aspects. Holistic development is concerned with ensuring that educational experiences contribute not only to academic knowledge but also to emotional intelligence, ethical values, creativity, and physical health, all for the betterment of the individual and society as a whole. Fulfillment comes from an education that empowers individuals to pursue their passions and interests, leading to a satisfying and balanced life.

- **Community and Connections:** This principle focuses on the importance of fostering a sense of belonging and interdependence within the educational environment. It involves creating a supportive network where all members feel valued, respected, and connected. For students, it means nurturing relationships with peers and teachers, and for educators, it involves collegiality and collaboration with fellow staff and the community at large. This tenet holds that education should be both a personal journey and a communal experience that encourages empathy, healthy relationships, cooperation, and active participation in the wider community.

- **Agency and Autonomy:** This tenet is concerned with the empowerment of individuals to take control of their learning, academic practices, endeavors, and development. Students are encouraged to be self-directed, make choices about their learning paths, and be active participants in their education. Teachers are supported and given the freedom and respect to exercise professional discretion, innovate in their teaching, and make decisions that best serve the needs of their students. This tenet asserts that a sense of ownership and self-determination is critical for deep learning as well as personal and professional fulfillment and growth.

- **Ethical Responsibility:** Ethical responsibility underlines the moral obligations of all stakeholders—students, teachers, administrators, and the community. This involves teaching and modeling values such as integrity, dignity, fairness, respect, and care for others. It also encompasses committing to social responsibility and justice, recognizing and addressing inequalities, and striving for a more equitable and just society. This tenet implies that education has a role in shaping conscientious citizens who are aware of their impact on the environment and world and act with consideration for the greater good.

- **Responsive and Adaptive Systems:** Education systems need to be responsive to the changing needs of students, educators, and society.

This means having policies, curricula, and practices that are flexible and can be tailored to address individual and collective needs. It also involves being open to new ideas, integrating feedback, and making necessary adjustments in a timely manner. For learners and teachers alike, this tenet ensures that the education system remains relevant, effective, and capable of supporting their evolving goals and circumstances.

These pillars and tenets weave together to form the fabric of an educational system dedicated to more than just the transmission of knowledge; they seek to foster a rich tapestry of growth, community spirit, innovation, and ethical conduct. They underscore the commitment to nurturing an ecosystem where both learners and educators not only thrive but also contribute meaningfully to a responsible and sustainable future. This framework advocates for a holistic educational journey—one that not only imparts cognitive skills but also cultivates emotional, social, and moral competencies, preparing all individuals to navigate and lead in a complex, interconnected world. In championing these principles, the goal is to transform education into a dynamic, equitable, and sustainable force for good, positioning it as a cornerstone of societal well-being and progress.

REFERENCES

Aker, M., Pentón Herrera, L. J., & Daniel, L. (2018). Back to the future: The implications of service and problem-based learning in the language, literacy, and cultural acquisition of ESOL students in the 21st century. *The Reading Matrix: An International Online Journal, 18*(2), 165–181.

Alber, D. (2021). *A little SPOT of feelings and emotions: Educator's guide*. Diane Alber Art LLC.

Alemdar, M., & Anılan, H. (2020). The development and validation of the emotional literacy skills scale. *International Journal of Contemporary Educational Research, 7*(2), 258–270. https://doi.org/10.33200/ijcer.757853

Anderson, M. (2022, September 26). How social-emotional learning became a frontline in the battle against CRT. NPR. https://www.npr.org/2022/09/26/1124082878/how-social-emotional-learning-became-a-frontline-in-the-battle-against-crt

Ardi, P., Sari, R., Hidayat, L. E., Dewi, O. T. S., & Cahyono, B. Y. (2023). In-service EFL teachers' well-being during online teacher professional development program in Indonesia: An ecological perspective. *Studies in Linguistics, Culture, and FLT, 11*(2), 26–45. https://doi.org/10.46687/UUHH4920

Arnold, J., & Brown, H. D. (1999). A map of the terrain. In J. Arnold (Ed.), *Affect in language learning* (pp. 1–24). Cambridge University Press.

Ashdown, D. M., & Bernard, M. E. (2012). Can explicit instruction in social and emotional learning skills benefit the social-emotional development, well-being, and academic achievement of young children? *Early Childhood Education Journal, 39*(6), 397–405. https://doi.org/10.1007/s10643-011-0481-x

Bai, B., Shen, B., & Wang, J. (2021). Impacts of social and emotional learning (SEL) on English learning achievements in Hong Kong secondary schools. *Language Teaching Research*, 1–25. Online advanced publication. https://doi-org.proxygw.wrlc.org/10.1177/13621688211021736

Beard, K. S., Vakil, J. B., Chao, T., & Hilty, C. D. (2023). Time for change: Understanding teacher social-emotional learning supports for anti-racism and student well-being during COVID-19, and beyond. *Education and Urban Society, 55*(7), 825–843. https://doi.org/10.1177/00131245211062527

Beck, M., & Libert, B. (2017, February 15). The rise of AI makes emotional intelligence more important. *Harvard Business Review.* https://hbr.org/2017/02/the-rise-of-ai-makes-emotional-intelligence-more-important

Berger, C. (2023, September 8). The housing affordability crisis is a hidden reason your kid doesn't have a teacher—stunning report shows teachers can only afford 12% of homes near their work. *Fortune.* https://fortune.com/2023/09/08/housing-market-teacher-shortage-affordability-crisis-redfin-low-salaries/

Bezzina, A., & Camilleri, S. (2021). "Happy Children": A project that has the aim of developing emotional literacy and conflict resolution skills: A Maltese Case Study. *Pastoral Care in Education, 39*(1), 48–66. https://doi.org/10.1080/02643944.2020.1774633

Birch, B. (Ed.). (2022). *Creating classrooms of peace in English language teaching.* Routledge.

Birch, B. M. (2009). *The English language teacher in global civil society.* Routledge.

Brackett, M. (2019). *Permission to feel: Unlocking the power of emotions to help our kids, ourselves, and our society thrive.* Celadon Books.

Cahnmann-Taylor, M., & McGovern, K. (2021). *Enlivening instruction with drama and improv: A guide for second language and world language teachers.* Routledge.

Chambers, R. (1997). Editorial: Responsible well-being—A personal agenda for development. *World Development, 25*(11), 1743–1754. https://doi.org/10.1016/S0305-750X(97)10001-8

Chandler, A. (2022). *The flexible SEL classroom: Practical ways to build social emotional learning* (2nd ed.). Routledge.

Chatterjee Singh, N., & Duraiappah, A. K. (Eds.). (2020). *Rethinking learning: A review of social and emotional learning frameworks for education systems.* UNESCO MGIEP.

Cheng, X., Xie, H., Hong, J., Bao, G., & Liu, Z. (2022). Teacher's emotional display affects students' perceptions of teacher's competence, feelings, and productivity in online small-group discussions. *Frontiers in Psychology, 12,* 795708. https://doi.org/10.3389/fpsyg.2021.795708

Cohen, J., Mccabe, E. M., Michelli, N. M., & Pickeral, T. (2009). School climate: Research, policy, practice, and teacher education. *Teachers College Record, 111*(1), 180–213. https://doi.org/10.1177/016146810911100108

Collaborative for Academic, Social, and Emotional Learning. (CASEL). (n.d.). About CASEL: Our history. https://casel.org/about-us/our-history/

Comer, J. P. (1980). *School power: Implications of an intervention project. With a new preface and epilogue.* Free Press.

Comer, J. P., & Emmons, C. (2006). The research program of the Yale Child Study Center School Development Program. *The Journal of Negro Education, 75*(3), 353–372.

Cope, B., & Kalantzis, M. (Eds.). (2000). *Multiliteracies: Literacy learning and the design of social futures.* Routledge.

Darragh, J., & Pentón Herrera, L. J. (2023). *2023 Specialist master class: Social-emotional learning and trauma-sensitive practices.* https://www.youtube.com/watch?v=tg5HFugz67w&list=PL_IwQaokU3YrhOhOzb23BPFPUCZbHaULn

Devaney, E., & Moroney, D. A. (Eds.). (2018). *Social and emotional learning in out-of-school time: Foundations and futures.* Information Age Publishing.

Durlak, J. A., Weissberg, R. P., Dymnicki, A. B., Taylor, R. D., & Schellinger, K. B. (2011). The impact of enhancing students' social and emotional learning: A meta-analysis of school-based universal interventions. *Child Development, 82*(1), 405–432. https://doi.org/10.1111/j.1467-8624.2010.01564.x

Eisenstein, E. L. (1980). *The printing press as an agent of change.* Cambridge University Press.

Elias, M. J., Zins, J. E., Weissberg, R. P., Frey, K. S., Greenberg, M. T., Haynes, N. M., Kessler, R., Schwab-Stone, M. E., & Shriver, T. P. (1997). *Promoting social and emotional learning: Guidelines for educators.* ASCD.

Feryok, A. (Ed.). (2024). *Language teacher identity and wellbeing.* Multilingual Matters.

Freire, P. (2000). *Pedagogy of the oppressed: 30th anniversary edition.* Continuum.

Gilster, P. (1997). *Digital literacy.* John Wiley & Sons, Inc.

Giroux, L. N. (2022). *Create an emotion-rich classroom: Helping young children build their social emotional skills.* Free Spirit Publishing.

Goleman, D. (1998). *Working with emotional intelligence.* Bantam Press.

Goleman, D. (2005). *Emotional intelligence: Why it can matter more than IQ.* Bantam Books.

Gottfredson, R. K., & Becker, W. J. (2023). How past trauma impacts emotional intelligence: Examining the connection. *Frontiers in Psychology, 14*, 1067509. https://doi.org/10.3389/fpsyg.2023.1067509

Hall, J., K., & Eggington, W. G. (Eds.). (2000). *The sociopolitics of English language teaching.* Multilingual Matters.

Hasper, A. (2023, March 19). Social and emotional learning skills for your classroom. *Cambridge: World of Better Learning Blog.* https://www.cambridge.org/elt/blog/2023/03/19/social-emotional-learning-skills-your-classroom/

Hobbs, R. (2010). *Digital and media literacy: A plan of action.* The Aspen Institute.

Horwitz, E. K. (1996). Even teachers get the blues: Recognizing and alleviating language teachers' feeling of foreign language anxiety. *Foreign Language Annals, 29*(3), 365–372. https://doi.org/10.1111/j.1944-9720.1996.tb01248.x

Hymes, D. H. (1972). On communicative competence. In J. B. Pride & J. Holmes (Eds.), *Sociolinguistics: Selected readings* (pp. 269–293). Penguin.

Kao, G. (1999). Psychological well-being and educational achievement among immigrant youth. In D. J. Hernandez (Ed.), *Children of immigrants: Health, adjustment, and public assistance* (pp. 410–477). National Academy Press.

Karam, F. J. (2021). Re-envisioning the ESOL classroom through a virtues-based curriculum: Contributions to critical dialogic education. *TESOL Journal, 12*(3), e582. https://doi.org/10.1002/tesj.582

Keyes, C. L. M. (1998). Social well-being. *Social Psychology Quarterly, 61*(2), 121–140.

Kovats Sánchez, G., Mesinas, M., Casanova, S., Barillas Chón, D. W., & Pentón Herrera, L. J. (2022). Creating positive learning communities for diasporic Indigenous students. *Journal of Multilingual and Multicultural Development.* Ahead of Print. https://doi.org/10.1080/01434632.2022.2159033

Krashen, S. D. (1982). *Principles and practice in second language acquisition.* Pergamon Press.

Kumaravadivelu, B. (2006). *Understanding language teaching: From method to postmethod.* Lawrence Erlbaum.

Ladd, A. (2003). Emotional literacy and healthy relationships. In R. DeMaria, M. T. Hannah, & L. Gordon (Eds.), *Building intimate relationships: Bridging treatment, education, and enrichment through the PAIRS program* (pp. 77–93). Brunner-Routledge.

Langer, J. A. (2014). Literacy and schooling: A sociocognitive perspective. In E. H. Hiebert (Ed.), *Literacy for a diverse society: Perspectives, practices, and policies* (pp. 9–27). TextProject, Inc.

Larsen-Freeman, D., & Anderson, M. (2011). *Techniques and principles in language teaching* (3rd ed.). Oxford University Press.

Lewis, C., Perry, R., & Murata, A. (2006). How should research contribute to instructional improvement? The case of lesson study. *Educational Researcher, 35*(3), 3–14. https://doi.org/10.3102/0013189X035003003

Limone, P., & Toto, G. A. (2022). Psychological and emotional effects of digital technology on digitods (14–18 Years): A systematic review. *Frontiers in Psychology, 13*, 938965. https://doi.org/10.3389/fpsyg.2022.938965

Livingstone, S. (2004). Media literacy and the challenge of new information and communication technologies. *The Communication Review, 7*(1), 3–14. https://doi.org/10.1080/10714420490280152

MacIntyre, P. D., Gregersen, T., & Mercer, S. (2019). Setting an agenda for positive psychology in SLA: Theory, practice, and research. *The Modern Language Journal, 103*(1), 262–274. https://doi.org/10.1111/modl.12544

Madigan, D. J., & Kim, L. E. (2021). Does teacher burnout affect students? A systematic review of its association with academic achievement and student-reported outcomes. *International Journal of Educational Research, 105*, 101714. https://doi.org/10.1016/j.ijer.2020.101714

Malkoç, A., & Zeynep, A. S. (2020). The relationship between emotional literacy, cognitive flexibility, and counseling self-efficacy of senior students in psychology and psychological counseling and guidance. *Educational Research and Reviews, 15*(1), 27–33. https://doi.org/10.5897/ERR2019.3848

Martínez-Alba, G., & Pentón Herrera, L. J. (2023). Strength in storytelling: Peacebuilding via wordless books. *TESOL Journal, 14*(4), e735. https://doi.org/10.1002/tesj.735

Martínez-Alba, G., Pentón Herrera, L. J., & Trinh. E. (2023). Situating teacher well-being in English language teaching. In L. J. Pentón Herrera, G. Martínez-Alba, & E. Trinh (Eds.), *Teacher well-being in English language teaching: An ecological pathway* (pp. 29–42). Routledge.

Maslow, A. H. (1943). A theory of human motivation. *Psychological Review, 50*(4), 370–396. https://doi.org/10.1037/h0054346

Mayer, J. D., & Salovey, P. (1997). What is emotional intelligence? In P. Salovey, & D. J. Sluyter (Eds.), *Emotional development and emotional intelligence: Educational implications* (pp. 3–34). Basic Books.

McCormick, M. P., Cappella, E., O'Connor, E. E., & McClowry, S. G. (2015). Social-emotional learning and academic achievement: Using causal methods to explore classroom-level mechanisms. *AERA Open, 1*(3), 1–26. https://doi.org/10.1177/2332858415603959

McGovern, K. R., & Yeganeh, V. (2023). Drama for dialogue of civilizations: Performance as storytelling in the adult ESOL classroom. *TESOL Journal,* e745. https://doi.org/10.1002/tesj.745

McNair, R. L., & Pentón Herrera, L. J. (2022). Peacemaking circles in the English language classroom. In B. Birch (Ed.), *Creating classrooms of peace in English language teaching* (pp. 194–207). Routledge.

Mercer, S. (2021). An agenda for well-being in ELT: An ecological perspective. *ELT Journal, 75*(1), 14–21. https://doi.org/10.1093/elt/ccaa062

Mercer, S., & Dörnyei, Z. (2020). *Engaging language learners in contemporary classrooms.* Cambridge University Press.

Mercer, S., & Gregersen, T. (2020). *Teacher wellbeing.* Oxford University Press.

Mesinas, M., & Casanova, S. (2023). The value of communal and intergenerational settings for studying social and emotional learning. *Child Development Perspectives, 17*(3–4), 122–128. https://doi.org/10.1111/cdep.12485

Mesquita, B. (2022). *Between us: How cultures create emotions.* W. W. Norton.

Milanovic, N. (2023, May 16). Technology will change the world—Will the world change with it? *Forbes.* https://www.forbes.com/sites/nikmilanovic/2023/05/16/technology-will-change-the-worldwill-the-world-change-with-it/?sh=329c15f93364

Mishra, D. (2015). Will the spread of digital technologies spell the end of the knowledge divide? *Brookings Blum Roundtable.* https://www.brookings.edu/wp-content/uploads/2016/07/MishraEndoftheKnowledgeDivide.pdf

Mok, M. M. C. (2019). Social and emotional learning. *Educational Psychology, 39*(9), 1115–1118. https://doi.org/10.1080/01443410.2019.1654195

Moreira-Sarmiento, M. C., Cordero-Clavijo, A. M., Córdova-Tobar, N. J., & Quevedo-Jumbo, J. M., (2022). El bienestar emocional del docente y su incidencia en el desempeño académico dentro de la educación tecnológica. *Polo del Conocimiento, 7*(7), 140–159. http://dx.doi.org/10.23857/pc.v7i7.4216

Mueller, H., & Pentón Herrera, L. J. (2023). Nature journaling in English language teaching: An introduction for practitioners. *Innovation in Language Learning and Teaching*. https://doi.org/10.1080/17501229. 2023.2256050

Namaziandost, E., Rezai, A., Heydarnejad, T., & Kruk, M. (2023). Emotion and cognition are two wings of the same bird: Insights into academic emotion regulation, critical thinking, self-efficacy beliefs, academic resilience, and academic engagement in Iranian EFL context. *Thinking Skills and Creativity*. Early view. https://doi.org/10.1016/j.tsc.2023.101409

Osher, D., Kidron, Y., Brackett, M., Dymnicki, A., Jones, S., & Weissberg, R. P. (2016). Advancing the science and practice of social and emotional learning: Looking back and moving forward. *Review of Research in Education*, 40(1), 644–681. https://doi.org/10.3102/0091732x16673595

Peetz, C. (2023, June 23). Here's how educators feel about their safety at school. *Education Week*. https://www.edweek.org/leadership/heres-how-educators-feel-about-their-safety-at-school/2023/06

Pelin, R-Ș. (2021). The impact of English language learning on the acquisition of soft skills such as critical thinking and emotional literacy skills. *Lucrări Științifice*, 64(1), 41–46. https://repository.uaiasi.ro/xmlui/handle/20.500.12811/2992

Pennycook, A. (1989). The concept of method, interested knowledge, and the politics of language teaching. *TESOL Quarterly*, 23(4), 589–618. https://doi.org/10.2307/3587534

Pentón Herrera, L. J. (2019). How to behave and why: Exploring moral values and behavior in the ESOL newcomer classroom. *TESOL Quarterly*, 53(4), 1033–1059. https://doi.org/10.1002/tesq.532

Pentón Herrera, L. J. (2020). Social-emotional learning in TESOL: What, why, and how. *Journal of English Learner Education*, 10(1), 1–16.

Pentón Herrera, L. J. (2023). Social-emotional learning in ESOL with ninth-grade newcomers. *ELT Journal*, 78(2), 127–136. https://doi.org/10.1093/elt/ccad051

Pentón Herrera, L. J., & Martínez-Alba, G. (2021). *Social-emotional learning in the English language classroom: Fostering growth, self-care, and independence*. TESOL Press.

Pentón Herrera, L. J., & Martínez-Alba, G. (2022). Emotions, well-being, and language teacher identity development in an EFL teacher preparation program. *Korea TESOL Journal*, 18(1), 3–25.

Pentón Herrera, L. J., Martínez-Alba, G., & Trinh, E. T. (Eds.). (2023a). *Teacher well-being in English language teaching: An ecological approach.* Routledge.

Pentón Herrera, L. J., Martínez-Alba, G., & Trinh. E. (2023b). Teacher well-being in English language teaching: An ecological introduction. In L. J. Pentón Herrera, G. Martínez-Alba, & E. Trinh (Eds.), *Teacher well-being in English language teaching: An ecological approach* (pp. 1–9). Routledge.

Pentón Herrera, L. J., & McNair, R. L. (2021). Restorative and community-building practices as social justice for English learners. *TESOL Journal,* 12(1), 1–11. https://doi.org/10.1002/tesj.523

Pritchard, M. E., & Wilson, G. S. S. (2003). Using emotional and social factors to predict student success. *Journal of College Student Development,* 44(1), 18–28. https://doi.org/10.1353/csd.2003.0008

Richards, J. C. (2022). Exploring Emotions in Language Teaching. *RELC Journal,* 53(1), 225–239. https://doi.org/10.1177/0033688220927531

Richards, J. C., & Rodgers, T. S. (2001). *Approaches and methods in language teaching* (2nd ed.). Cambridge University Press.

Ryff, C. D. (1989). Happiness is everything, or is it? Explorations on the meaning of psychological well-being. *Journal of Personality and Social Psychology,* 57(6), 1069–1081. https://doi.org/10.1037/0022-3514.57.6.1069

Ryff, C. D., & Keyes, C. L. (1995). The structure of psychological well-being revisited. Journal of Personality and Social Psychology, 69(4), 719–727. https://doi.org/10.1037//0022-3514.69.4.719

Saarni, C. (1999). *The development of emotional competence.* The Guilford Press.

Salcedo, M. (2018). *Uncover the roots of challenging behavior: Create responsive environments where young children thrive.* Free Spirit Publishing.

Schutz, P. A., & Pekrun, R. (Eds.). (2007). *Emotion in education.* Elsevier Academic Press.

Soodmand Afshar, H., & Rahimi, M. (2016). Reflective thinking, emotional intelligence, and speaking ability of EFL learners: Is there a relation? *Thinking Skills and Creativity,* 19, 97–11. https://doi.org/10.1016/j.tsc.2015.10.005

Soodmand Afshar, H., Tofighi, S., & Hamazavi, R. (2016). Iranian EFL learners' emotional intelligence, learning styles, strategy use, and their L2 achievement. *Issues in Educational Research,* 26(4), 635–652.

Sotiriadis, M., & Galanakis, M. (2022). Self-regulation and emotional resilience in the workplace: A systematic review. *Psychology Research, 12*(1), 957–964. https://doi.org/10.17265/2159-5542/2022.12.007

Srikanth, S., & Sonawat, R. (2012). Emotional literacy: The ABC of understanding emotions. *Indian Journal of Positive Psychology, 3*(3), 309–316.

Steiner, C. (2003). *Emotional literacy: Intelligence with a heart.* Personhood Press.

Steiner, C., & Perry, P. (1997). *Achieving emotional literacy: A personal program to increase your emotional intelligence.* Bloomsbury.

Strauss, V. (2023, January 26). The basic rights teachers don't have. *The Washington Post.* https://www.washingtonpost.com/education/2023/01/26/basic-rights-teachers-dont-have/

Street, B. V. (1984). *Literacy in theory and practice.* Cambridge University Press.

Suganda, L. A., Petrus, I., Zuraida Z., & Kurniawan, D. (2018). A study on the creative social emotional learning English (CSELE) classroom model in Indonesian context. *The Journal of English Literacy Education, 5*(1), 34–41. https://doi.org/10.36706/jele.v5i1.5927

Tao, J., & Gao, X. (2021). *Language teacher agency.* Cambridge University Press.

Tierney, R. J., & Pearson, P. D. (2021). *A history of literacy education: Waves of research and practice.* Teachers College Press.

Tyng, C. M., Amin, H. U., Saad, M. N. M., & Malik, A. S. (2017). The influences of emotion on learning and memory. *Frontiers in Psychology, 8*, 1454. https://doi.org/10.3389/fpsyg.2017.01454

Wang, H., Wang, Y., & Li, S. (2023). Unpacking the relationships between emotions and achievement of EFL learners in China: Engagement as a mediator. *Frontiers in Psychology, 14*, 1098916. https://doi.org/10.3389/fpsyg.2023.1098916

Waterhouse, A. (2019). *Emotional literacy: Supporting emotional health and wellbeing in school.* Routledge.

White, C. J. (2018). The emotional turn in applied linguistics and TESOL: Significance, challenges and prospects. In J. de D. Martínez Agudo (Ed.), *Emotions in second language teaching: Theory, research, and teacher education* (pp. 19–34). Springer. https://doi.org/10.1007/978-3-319-75438-3_2

Yazan, B. (2019). Toward identity-oriented teacher education: Critical autoethnographic narrative. *TESOL Journal, 10*(1), e00388. https://doi.org/10.1002/tesj.388

Yazan, B., Trinh, E. T., & Pentón Herrera, L. J. (Eds.). (2023). *Doctoral students' identities and emotional wellbeing in applied linguistics: Autoethnographic accounts.* Routledge.

Žydžiūnaitė, V., & Daugėla, M. (2020). Teacher's professional self-awareness within the interactions with students in higher education: Temporality and relationality. *Acta Paedagogica Vilnensia, 45,* 160–174. https://doi.org/10.15388/ActPaed.45.10